Grammar Dimensions
Workbook Four

Gene Parulis

Heinle & Heinle Publishers

I(T)P **An International Thomson Publishing Company**

Boston, Massachusetts 02116 U.S.A.

Photos on: page 66, page 67 (top and middle): Jonathan Stark, photo/video specialist, Heinle & Heinle Publishers; page 67 (bottom): courtesy of Stock, Boston, Inc.

10 9 8 7 6 5 4 3 2

Table of Contents

UNIT

Verb Tenses in Discourse

EXERCISE 1   (*Focus 1*)

Fill in each blank with the correct form of the verb in parentheses.

(1) Five years ago, Raul _____ (arrive) in this country. (2) He _____ (never be) here before. (3) At the moment, he _____ (study) computer science. (4) He _____ (expect) that he _____ (work) as a programmer in another year. (5) "If that job _____ (not work out)," he told me, "I _____ (go) back to school in another field."

(6) For the last two years, he _____ (live) in a small museum as a caretaker. (7) He _____ (have) a tiny room of his own, but when the museum _____ (close), he _____ (have) the whole place to himself. (8) The only time I _____ (ever be) to a party in a museum _____ (be) when Raul _____ (invite) me a few weeks ago.

(9) "_____ (ever thought) about returning home?" I asked him the other day. (10) "Maybe, someday, I _____ (go) back," he said, "but only to visit."

(11) He said last week he _____ (speak) briefly to his brother who _____ (try) for months to get a visa. (12) Apparently, his brother _____ (give up).

(13) This coming January, I _____ (know) Raul for three years.

The following passage is from a popular novel, *The Kitchen God's Wife*, by Amy Tan. Cover the original version, which appears below, and then fill in the blanks with the correct verb tenses. After you have done that compare the original with your own work. How do you explain any differences?

And then there is my cousin Bao-bao, whose real name is Roger. Everyone in the family

_____ (call) him Bao-bao ever since he _____ (be) a baby,

which _____ (be) what *bao-bao* _____ (mean)—"precious

baby." Later, we _____ (keep) calling him that because he

_____ (be) the crybaby who always _____ (wail) the minute

my aunt and uncle _____ (walk) in the door, claiming we other kids

_____ (pick) on him. And even though he _____ (be) now

thirty-one years old, we still _____ (think) of him as Bao-bao—and we

_____ (be) still _____ (pick) on him.

Original

And then there is my cousin Bao-bao, whose real name is Roger. Everyone in the family has been calling him Bao-bao ever since he was a baby, which is what *bao-bao* means—"precious baby." Later, we kept calling him that because he was the crybaby who always wailed the minute my aunt and uncle walked in the door, claiming we other kids had been picking on him. And even though he's now thirty-one years old, we still think of him as Bao-bao—and we're still picking on him.

EXPLANATION OF DIFFERENCES:

_____

_____

_____

_____

_____

_____

_____

_____

_____

_____

EXERCISE 3 (Focus 2)

Complete the following sentences in your own words.

1. When I was younger _____

2. By the year 2020 _____

3. At 3 P.M. yesterday _____

4. Since I last saw Marion _____

5. At this very moment _____

6. During the reign of Kublai Khan _____

7. In the coming century _____

8. Just a minute ago _____

9. After I graduate _____

10. After the last ice age _____

11. For the last ten years _____

12. In 1066 _____

13. By the time my parents see this report _____

14. This year _____

15. Tomorrow evening _____

EXERCISE 4 (Focus 3)

Each of the following passages has one sentence with a verb tense that is inappropriate in the context. Identify those sentences and correct them.

1. **(a)** The earth is the fifth largest planet and the third from the sun. **(b)** It is the only planet in the solar system known to have water. **(c)** Its day length, caused by its rotation, is between that of Neptune (16 hours) and that of Mars (24.5 hours).
   (d) Earth's seasons are caused by its tilt; when the north pole of the planet is pointed toward the sun, it will be summer in the northern hemisphere, and when it points away, it will be winter.

2. **(a)** The moon is larger than Pluto, the smallest planet in the solar system. **(b)** Its rotation takes exactly the same time as its orbit around the earth; thus it always shows the same side to the earth. **(c)** The moon wasn't solely responsible for raising and lowering the oceans of the earth, but its pull is 2.2 times greater than that of the sun.

3. **(a)** Pluto's orbit is so irregular that it is now inside of Neptune's orbit. **(b)** Only after 1999 will Pluto be the farthest planet from the sun again. **(c)** Pluto took almost 248 earth years to go around the sun. **(d)** It rotates once every 6.4 days.

4. **(a)** Mercury is the second smallest planet in our solar system. **(b)** Because Mercury is so close to the sun, its year takes only 88 earth days. **(c)** However, Mercury rotates much more slowly than Earth, so a day on Mercury will take almost 59 earth days; thus its year is less than two Mercury days long.

5. **(a)** Predicting the movements of the planets was important to many past cultures, who believed that their fates were related to those of the planets. **(b)** Today many cultures still follow the movements of the planets and have paid special attention to their positions on important days such as births, deaths, and anniversaries.

6. **(a)** The planets retained a special influence over our collective imagination.
(b) Countless love poems deal with the moon and the planets—one of which, Venus, is also the name of the goddess of love. **(c)** And no pair of lovers can fail to appreciate the beauty of a full moon in a clear sky.

7. **(a)** We were discussing sports the other day. **(b)** Rob said he loved baseball. **(c)** Mary said she had always been crazy about soccer. **(d)** Tim plays basketball.

8. **(a)** We were amazed at the number of species we see in Costa Rica: 71 types of birds, plus monkeys, crocodiles, frogs, turtles, butterflies, and plants. **(b)** It was a wonderful experience that I will never forget.

9. **(a)** On the cruise you will be able to eat any time you want. **(b)** You will have opportunities to explore ancient ports and ruins and listen to lectures by expert guides. **(c)** You will have enjoyed the trip immensely.

10. **(a)** A passion for hiking has long kept Czechs on the move—their national hiking club dates from 1888. **(b)** Partly inspired by the June 1990 issue of *National Geographic* magazine, Czechs and Austrians create the Czech Greenway, a 250-mile network of trails between Vienna and Prague. **(c)** Traversable by foot, bicycle, horseback, or canoe, the system connects medieval castles and towns with the countryside.

Circle the correct verb forms in the following passages.

1. I'm sitting in the living room of my grandparents' home. I (**a.** am not **b.** haven't been **c.** wasn't) here in years. I (**a.** remember **b.** have remembered **c.** remembered) how dark and large and full of strange furniture the room was when I (**a.** am **b.** have been **c.** was) a child. The room (**a.** is **b.** has been **c.** was) ideal for playing hide and seek. Though it's the same room with mostly the same furniture, it (**a.** seems **b.** has seemed **c.** seemed) to have shrunk.

2. "I graduate from high school next week. Next year I (**a.** go **b.** will go **c.** will have gone) to community college. I (**a.** take **b.** am taking **c.** will take) some computer classes, I think, but I'm not sure what I (**a.** do **b.** am doing **c.** will do) with the rest of my life! Everything today (**a.** has **b.** is having **c.** will have) to do with computers. My dad says that if I learn how to use one, he (**a.** buys **b.** is buying **c.** will buy) me one.

   I used to go to a certain high school, but I (**a.** have gotten **b.** get **c.** was getting) straight Fs. My parents (**a.** switch **b.** have switched **c.** switched) me to another school; I (**a.** get **b.** have gotten **c.** got) As and Bs now. The new school (**a.** helped **b.** has helped **c.** helps) me a lot. In the old school I (**a.** go **b.** was going **c.** have gone) nowhere."

   (Adapted from Gordon Mathews, *What Makes Life Worth Living? How Japanese and Americans Make Sense of Their World.* Berkeley: University of California Press, 1996, p. 111.)

3. "My wife is a real support to me. One night I (**a.** look **b.** have looked **c.** looked) at her, and at our kids sleeping beside us. She (**a.** look **b.** have looked **c.** looked) so tired from taking care of them—I (**a.** feel **b.** have felt **c.** felt) I couldn't quit my company, however much I hated it. Later I did tell her I (**a.** want **b.** have wanted **c.** wanted) to quit; she said, 'Go ahead.' When I (**a.** ask **b.** have asked **c.** asked) her how we'd eat, she said we'd go to her parents' farm to live. If we could really do that, it'd be great.

   In this country, most husbands don't listen to their wives; they just (**a.** gave **b.** give **c.** have given) orders, so their wives (**a.** became **b.** become **c.** will become) like dolls, deprived of their own feelings. I'm lucky my wife (**a.** was not **b.** is not **c.** has not been) like that."

   (Adapted from Gordon Mathews, *What Makes Life Worth Living? How Japanese and Americans Make Sense of Their World.* Berkeley: University of California Press, 1996, p. 84.)

4. "I (**a.** am writing **b.** was writing **c.** have been writing) this column for ten years and, in that time, the numbers of subscribers to the magazine has more than tripled. Most of today's readers (**a.** probably never read **b.** are probably never reading **c.** have probably never read) the basic information that I (**a.** have written **b.** wrote **c.** write) about ten years ago. It (**a.** was **b.** has been **c.** is) all too easy to forget that the things I do automatically, after

decades of photography, may be unknown to someone just starting out. I (**a.** am also learning **b.** also learned **c.** have also learned) many new things in the past ten years that can be shared with new and old readers of my column.

To find wildlife, you must know wildlife, and there is no better way of knowing wildlife than living with it. Raised on a farm in the hills of northwestern New Jersey, I (**a.** hunt and roam **b.** have hunted and roamed **c.** hunted and roamed) the fields and woods around the Delaware River since age 11. Even before that, I read about wildlife, observing it and taking notes, and I still (**a.** do **b.** did **c.** have done) that today."

(Adapted from Leonard Lee Rue III, "Finding Wildlife," *Outdoor Photographer*, June 1996, p. 18.)

5. "As you journey through the lush, unspoiled western coast of British Columbia, before long you'll come upon a mystical white apparition—a white bear. Called "Spirit Bear" or "Ghost Bear" by the native Kitasoo who (**a.** are living **b.** lived **c.** have lived) here for thousands of years, this gentle variation of the black bear (**a.** wasn't **b.** isn't **c.** hasn't been) an albino. It (**a.** got **b.** gets **c.** has gotten) its pure white coat from a double recessive gene for white hair.

A Kitasoo legend tells of Raven, the Creator of all life, deciding to turn every tenth bear white to evoke memories of when ice and snow (**a.** cover **b.** covered **c.** has covered) the land. We now (**a.** knew **b.** know **c.** have known) this last ice age (**a.** ends **b.** ended **c.** has ended) 10,000 years ago. And when Raven (**a.** did **b.** does **c.** has done **d.** had done) his magic, he (**a.** issued **b.** issues **c.** had issued) a proclamation: Moksgm'ol, the white bear, (**a.** will live **b.** would live **c.** is living **d.** has been living) in this place, in peace, forever."

(Adapted from James Lawrence, "Spirit Bear," *Outdoor Photographer*, June 1996, pp. 40–41.)

6. Ask renowned nature photographer David Muench for the formula behind *Ancient America*'s magic and you'll get a deceptively simple answer: Prepare thoroughly. Go to the sacred places. Wait. Look. Feel. Then shoot.

But the art of David Muench's photography (**a.** has never been painted **b.** is never painted **c.** was never painted) solely with the tools of location, light, pattern, texture, color or technical mastery. He also (**a.** has known **b.** knows **c.** knew) how to let the miracles happen.

The seed of *Ancient America* (**a.** has been planted **b.** is planted **c.** was planted) in Muench's mind at the foot of a four-thousand-year-old bristlecone pine. "I always (**a.** have wanted **b.** want **c.** wanted) to do something with bristlecones," he recalls. "That desire (**a.** has expanded **b.** expands **c.** expanded) to the largest and the tallest trees, the sequoias and redwoods. And it (**a.** has gelled and formulated **b.** gels and formulates **c.** gelled and formulated) in my mind for maybe ten years or more. Nowadays, everything (**a.** has been becoming **b.** is becoming **c.** was becoming) so technical in the world. I (**a.** have felt **b.** feel **c.** felt) it was important with the book to touch on something vitally important—our natural beginnings. I (**a.** am not sitting **b.** was not sitting **c.** haven't been sitting) in judgment, but rather wanting to make sure we don't lose the purest sense of our natural world."

(Adapted from James Lawrence, "Ancient America," *Outdoor Photographer*, June 1996, pp. 30–36.)

EXERCISE 6   (*Focus 4*)

Rewrite this description of a past event in the present tense to make it seem more immediate.

A student took an exam in a large lecture course with over 300 students. At the end of the period, the professor announced that time was up, and the students had to turn in their exams. All the students came to the front and put their exams in a pile, except for one student who remained at his seat for 10 extra minutes furiously filling in answers. When the student came to the front to hand in the exam, the professor told him that his grade would be lowered for taking too much time. Suddenly the student stiffened and indignantly asked the professor, "Do you know who I am?" The surprised professor replied, "No." The student replied, "Good!" and with one quick motion, lifted the huge pile of papers and placed his in the middle.

_____

_____

_____

_____

_____

_____

_____

_____

_____

_____

_____

_____

_____

Read the story below once or twice and then cover it up. In the space provided rewrite the story in your own words using the present tense.

Four students sharing a dormitory room stayed out late one night and were too tired to get up in time for their early class the next morning. On the way to school, they all agreed on an excuse to tell their professor. They arrived near the end of class, and went up to the professor to ask if they could make up the day's quiz. The professor asked them why they were late, and they told him that it was because they had had a flat tire on the way to school. The professor told them to take their seats in separate corners of the room and each take out a sheet of paper for their quiz. He then asked them each to write down which tire was flat.

UNIT 2 Verbs
Aspect and Time Frames

Fill in the blanks with simple present, simple future, or simple past forms of the verbs in parentheses as appropriate.

1. I _____ (have) two beautiful Siamese cats once.

2. Our office _____ (contact) you first thing in the morning. Don't leave until you hear from us.

3. Chlorophyll _____ (make) leaves green.

4. In those days we _____ (decorate) eggs for Easter, using many different colors.

5. Come January, we _____ (own) our house outright and no longer be mortgaged to the bank.

6. We _____ (think) we _____ (see) a ghost on the stairway but it was only the moonlight and a puff of dust from a cracked window.

7. The latest figures _____ (reveal) that the average American family has pizza at least once a week.

8. When I get to college, I _____ (spend) a half hour every day writing in my journal.

9. Buy the new improved Nutri-Milk. Every serving _____ (give) a full day's supply of vitamin C and calcium.

10. I _____ (believe) you only when you present me with incontrovertible proof.

Decide whether a simple tense or a progressive tense is appropriate for each verb in parentheses and fill in the blanks including any adverbs given.

1. Do you **(a)** _____ (wonder) how to get into the best companies or how to accelerate your rise to management? Many employers say they

(b) _____ (look for) people who **(c)** _____ (have) an

MBA degree in addition to their technical credentials.

Major firms often **(d)** _____ (look) more closely at technical people with advanced management degrees. Some firms expressly **(e)** _____ (ask) for upper-level degrees. According to one corporate recruiter, graduate management degree holders **(f)** _____ (understand) not just how products are made, but also how corporations **(g)** _____ (work).

Stephanie Tran **(h)** _____ (believe) that her master's degree in information systems has helped her greatly. She **(i)** _____ (feel) that the degree **(j)** _____ (give) her a view of how technology is used in business.

For example, Stephanie **(k)** _____ (write, currently) the specifications and instructions for a new system. Her technical knowledge **(l)** _____ (provide) the detail the documentation needs. Her business knowledge **(m)** _____ (help) her understand the needs of the workers using the system. She **(n)** _____ (look, also) to the future for new and efficient technical standards the company might want to adopt.

2. As she and her friends **(a)** _____ (talk) about the classes they **(b)** _____ (want) to take next semester, Lin **(c)** _____ (notice) that Sang **(d)** _____ (seem) sad. When she **(e)** _____ (ask) him what was wrong, he **(f)** _____ (tell) her that he **(g)** _____ (have) doubts about next semester. Although he **(h)** _____ (go) to school full-time last semester, he **(i)** _____ (run) his sick father's business now, and he rarely **(j)** _____ (have) enough time to study.

3. Right now Tran **(a)** _____ (study) English at a community college. She **(b)** _____ (hope) to transfer to a four-year college and study electrical engineering. She **(c)** _____ (be) the first in her family to go to college, and so she **(d)** _____ (feel) a lot of pressure not to fail. She **(e)** _____ (have) very supportive parents, though, who **(f)** _____ (do, constantly) everything they can to encourage her. Her mother often **(g)** _____ (mail) her presents from home, and her father **(h)** _____ (tell, always) her how proud he **(i)** _____ (be) of her.

4. Kim **(a)** _____ (have) an RN degree, but she **(b)** _____ (work) as a waitress until her English

(c) _____ (improve) enough for her to pass her nursing exam. Every day Kim **(d)** _____ (work) from ten in the morning until late at night, sometimes until one or two o'clock. She **(e)** _____ (be) so tired when she gets home that she just **(f)** _____ (take) a shower while her dinner **(g)** _____ (cook), **(h)** _____ (eat) dinner, and **(i)** _____ (go) to bed without any time to study. She **(j)** _____ (realize) that her schedule **(k)** _____ (take) away her opportunities to improve herself, but she really **(l)** _____ (need) the money.

EXERCISE 3 (Focus 3)

Fill in each blank with either a simple or a perfect form of the verb in parentheses. More than one answer may be possible. Be prepared to explain your choices.

For years many Americans **(1)** _____ (believe) that somewhere between the ages of 40 and 60 people **(2)** _____ (suffer) something called a "midlife crisis." This **(3)** _____ (be) the feeling that youth **(4)** _____ (be) permanently behind, and only old age **(5)** _____ (lie) ahead. The stereotypical response to a midlife crisis **(6)** _____ (involve) some attempt to regain youth, and indeed, there **(7)** _____ (be) many newspaper stories about women having plastic surgery and men having affairs with younger women.

However, some recent studies **(8)** _____ (place) doubt on this stereotype, particularly for people who **(9)** _____ (possess) certain traits. One research group **(10)** _____ (learn) that people who **(11)** _____ (be) happiest during their middle ages **(12)** _____ (look) honestly at themselves and **(13)** _____ (accept) the changes that **(14)** _____ (come) with age. At middle age, these people **(15)** _____ (understand) that they **(16)** _____ (have, not) the same strength or beauty they **(17)** _____ (have) when they **(18)** _____ (be) twenty. So instead of relying on their physical qualities, at midlife these people **(19)** _____ (learn) to use the skills and wisdom the years **(20)** _____ (give) them. Often they use these qualities in ways that they **(21)** _____ (not consider) before. Women especially **(22)** _____ (tend) to find surprising strengths in themselves at middle age. For example, the writers Kate Chopin and Edith Wharton **(23)** _____ (not publish) anything before the age of 40.

Studies on relationships at middle age **(24)** _____ (find) a steady decline of stress in marriages all the way from youth into old age. Researchers **(25)** _____ (believe) that this **(26)** _____ (be) at least partly caused by what couples **(27)** _____ (learn) about each other when they are young. Finally, although in past studies middle-aged adults **(28)** _____ (score) lower than their younger counterparts on standardized cognitive tests, some researchers now **(29)** _____ (feel) that middle-aged people may simply see problems in equally intelligent but different ways from the young. Although they may not compute problems as quickly, middle-aged people **(30)** _____ (collect) more experience to base their solutions on. A young gardener might make a wonderful plan for his garden from the best books available, only to see his older neighbor's plot prosper from his greater knowledge of the weather and soil in that area.

EXERCISE 4   (*Focus 3*)

Study the excerpts below and select the correct form from the verb choices in parentheses.

1. **(A)** My work alone (**a.** has awarded   **b.** had awarded   **c.** will have awarded) me a top place and I was going to be one of the first called in the graduating ceremonies. On the classroom blackboard, as well as on the bulletin board in the auditorium, there were blue stars and white stars and red stars. No absences, no tardiness, and my academic work was among the best of the year.
   (B) My hair pleased me too. Gradually the black mass (**a.** has lengthened and thickened   **b.** had lengthened and thickened   **c.** was lengthening and thickening) so that it kept at last to its braided pattern and I didn't have to yank my scalp off when (**a.** have tried   **b.** had tried   **c.** tried) to comb it.
   (C) I hoped the memory of that morning would never leave me. Sunlight was itself young, and the day had none of the insistence maturity would bring it in a few hours. In my robe and barefoot in the backyard, under cover of going to see about my new beans, I gave myself up to the gentle warmth and thanked God that no matter what evil I (**a.** have done   **b.** had done   **c.** would have done) in my life, He (**a.** has allowed   **b.** had allowed   **c.** would have allowed) me to live to see this day.

   (From Maya Angelou, I *Know Why the Caged Bird Sings*. New York: Random House, 1969.)

2. **(A)** There was, however, one Italian import whose vocabulary (**a.** has had   **b.** had had   **c.** had) an influence on the language out of all proportion to its significance in the American-Italian community: the Mafia. **(B)** Now treated as synonymous with

organized crime (which it is not), the Mafia (**a.** has added   **b.** had added   **c.** added) terms like *godfather, the family,* and *capo* to the language. **(C)** Hollywood's love affair with "gangster movies" (**a.** has ensured   **b.** had ensured   **c.** ensured) a wide dissemination of criminal slang: *hoodlum, racketeer, rough house, hatchet man, doing the dirty work, hot seat* (originally "the electric chair"), *protection racket* and *loan shark.*

(From Robert McCrum, William Cran, and Robert MacNeil, *The Story of English*. New York: Viking, 1986.)

3. **(A)** The hallmark of the United States (**a.** has been   **b.** had been   **c.** was) growth. **(B)** Americans (**a.** have typically defined   **b.** had typically defined   **c.** typically defined) this process in quantitative terms. **(C)** Never (**a.** has been   **b.** had been   **c.** was) that more true than in the first half of the nineteenth century, when an unparalleled rate of growth took place in three dimensions: population, territory, and economy. **(D)** In 1850, Zachary Taylor—the last president born before the Constitution—could look back at vast changes during his adult life. **(E)** The population (**a.** has doubled   **b.** had doubled   **c.** doubled) and then doubled again. **(F)** Pushing relentlessly westward and southward, Americans (**a.** have similarly quadrupled   **b.** had similarly quadrupled   **c.** similarly quadrupled) the size of their country by settling, conquering, annexing, or purchasing territory that (**a.** has been occupied   **b.** had been occupied   **c.** was occupied) for millennia by Indians and claimed by France, Spain, Britain, and Mexico.

(From James M. McPherson, *Battle Cry of Freedom: The Civil War Era*. New York: Oxford University Press, 1988.)

EXERCISE 5   (Focus 3)

Fill in each blank with either the simple future or the future perfect form of each verb in parentheses.

College students have to compare the value of their degree with the time that is needed to obtain it. A medical student, for example, might say to herself, "When I graduate, I **(1)** _____ (be) 28 years old and **(2)** _____ (go) to college for over 12 years. I **(3)** _____ (spend) more than $75,000 on my education and **(4)** _____ (have) most of that amount in loans. **(5)** _____ (be, I) satisfied with my profession enough to justify those expenditures?" Some students feel that school alone does not guarantee their security or happiness; they worry that the job market **(6)** _____ (change) by the time they graduate, or that they **(7)** _____ (not have) enough work experience to compete for the best jobs, or that they **(8)** _____ (spend) a lot of time and money on their degree only to learn that they aren't satisfied with their career when they finally get a job. Therefore, more and more students are choosing to study part-time while they work or to include cooperative education in their degree programs so they can gain more job experience and a greater understanding of just what their careers **(9)** _____ (be) like.

EXERCISE 6 (Focus 4)

Decide whether the verbs in parentheses should express an action, event, or situation completed at a specific time in the past (simple past) or one that started in the past and continues to the present (present perfect or present perfect progressive). Write the appropriate form for each verb in the blank (more than one verb form may be appropriate for some blanks).

Lois and Omar **(1)** _____ (be) married since 1991. Five years ago they **(2)** _____ (move) to Chicago from Saint Louis. It **(3)** _____ (take) Lois two months to find a job but she finally **(4)** _____ (get) a position as a nurse's assistant. Omar **(5)** _____ (use) to play in a band when he **(6)** _____ (be) younger and he **(7)** _____ (find) work in a music store. For the last two years, Lois **(8)** _____ (work) at night and often on weekends too because she and Omar **(9)** _____ (try) to save enough money to buy a house. Interest rates **(10)** _____ (go) down recently, so Lois and Omar think that now is a good time to buy. They **(11)** _____ (look) at houses in the city, but decided that a house in the suburbs would be cheaper. Lately they **(12)** _____ (talk) to a real-estate agent about a house with a big yard near a friend of Lois. Their agent **(13)** _____ (plan) to sell the house to another couple, but the couple changed their minds and so now Lois and Omar have a chance.

Complete the crossword puzzle.

ACROSS

2. I am presently _____ on a paper about the impact of German immigration on the United States.

3. Mike _____ basketball every Friday with a bunch of old friends.

6. We haven't started yet. We _____ for the last two guests to arrive.

9. Over the last three years, Kim _____ in fourteen marathons.

11. Caffeine _____ most people.

12. Tex claims he's been playing the guitar _____ he was four. Do you know if it's true?

DOWN

1. Have you _____ washing the dishes yet?

3. The present progressive tense is made up of a present form of the verb *be* plus a _____ participle.

4. Ssssshhhhhh. The baby has _____ fallen asleep.

5. We _____ studying verb tenses for the last two weeks.

7. Sorry, Judy can't come to the phone now. She _____ a bath.

8. A leap year _____ every four years.

10. The present perfect tense is made up of *have* or *has* plus a _____ participle.

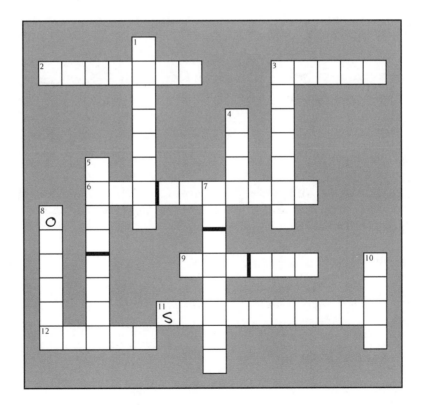

EXERCISE 8 (Focus 5)

Fill in each blank with either a simple present, a present progressive, a present perfect, or a present perfect progressive verb. More than one answer may be correct; be prepared to explain your choices.

Li Hong **(1)** _____ (feel) that her friends and her family **(2)** _____ (be) her two most important in-groups. She **(3)** _____ (be) close to about five friends for a long time. All of them **(4)** _____ (be) in the United States now, where two **(5)** _____ (study) nursing, and three **(6)** _____ (study) computer information systems. They **(7)** _____ (go) to three different schools in California, Virginia, and New York. They still **(8)** _____ (keep) in close contact with each other, though. In fact, Li Hong even **(9)** _____ (complain) a little about Yi Mei, who always **(10)** _____ (call) her up late at night while she **(11)** _____ (try) to study. For two years now, the friends **(12)** _____ (come) to Li Hong's house for Chinese New Year, since all their families **(13)** _____ (live, still) in Taiwan.

Li Hong's family **(14)** _____ (support) her both financially and emotionally during her stay in the United States. Her father often **(15)** _____ (send) her money and little letters of encouragement, while her mother frequently **(16)** _____ (mail) her small packages of food and **(17)** _____ (visit) her twice in the past two years. Li Hong especially **(18)** _____ (look forward) to her family's phone calls.

EXERCISE 9 (Focus 6)

Fill in each blanks with a simple present, simple past, past progressive, past perfect, or past perfect progressive form of the verb given. More than one answer may be possible; be prepared to explain your choices.

Many people **(1)** _____ (think) of dragons and heroes and monsters in the woods when they **(2)** _____ (hear) the word "legend." But there **(3)** _____ (be) other types of legends. Did you ever hear about the woman who **(4)** _____ (try) to dry her poodle in a microwave when the dog **(5)** _____ (explode)? Or the mysterious child hitchhiker that **(6)** _____ (appear) on a piece of road where a child **(7)** _____ (be) killed years earlier? If you **(8)** _____ (hear) any of these or other stories that just **(9)** _____ (sound) a little *too* interesting, you likely **(10)** _____ (hear) an urban legend.

American college campuses **(11)** _____ (host) a number of persistent urban legends over the years. Like legends from faraway places, these urban legends often **(12)** _____ (deal) with fantastic, grotesque, and odd occurrences. One famous legend **(13)** _____ (be) that the administration will give a student straight As if his or her roommate **(14)** _____ (commit) suicide. Other legends **(15)** _____ (concern) hidden lives of faculty members, such as the professor who **(16)** _____ (invent) a chemical warfare agent but **(17)** _____ (be) now prohibited from discussing it.

College students also **(18)** _____ (appear) in more common myths, such as the student on vacation who **(19)** _____ (drinking) and **(20)** _____ (wake) up the next day to find a scar on his back where his kidney **(21)** _____ (be). Another legend **(22)** _____ (concern) a student who **(23)** _____ (buy) a sports car from a woman for fifty dollars. The woman's husband **(24)** _____ (run) away with another woman and later **(25)** _____ (wrote) his wife, instructing her to sell his beloved sports car for whatever she could.

Interestingly, some urban legends **(26)** _____ (acquire) international status. Recently, an Internet discussion group **(27)** _____ (look) at urban legends from around the world. One story **(28)** _____ (concern) a little boy who **(29)** _____ (die) of some illness, and **(30)** _____ (need) to collect a huge number (say 10,000) of one essentially worthless item such as bottle caps or business cards to purchase an iron lung or other piece of medical equipment. Confirmation of this legend **(31)** _____ (come) from New Zealand, the United Kingdom, Israel, and Norway, among other places.

Complete the crossword puzzle.

ACROSS

2. Marcia will be _____ the office until Sydney gets back. Direct all questions to her.

7. Both the simple present and the present _____ can be used to refer to future time.

9. I_____ glad to give you a hand with your work this weekend.

10. I _____ to meet Susan on Wednesday.

DOWN

1. If you wait any longer, they _____ closed the gates by the time you get there.

3. By the time I finally finish college, my family will _____ nearly $100,000 for tuition, room & board, and other expenses. Where's the money going to come from?

4. When the green light _____ on above the door, call me right away.

5. In January, Emma will have been _____ on her Ph.D. for ten whole years.

6. The train for Richmond _____ from platform 3 in one hour.

8. Antonio _____ down to the carnival in Rio next week. I think he's taking Varig, the Brazilian national airline.

UNIT 3
Subject-Verb Agreement

EXERCISE 1 (*Focus 1*)

For each sentence below, identify the subject and circle its head noun. Then complete the sentence with a correct form of the verb.

EXAMPLE: The reading (habits) of a group ___*gives*___ (give) some measure of its intellectual activity.

The survey of American reading habits in your textbook **(1)** _____ (be) interesting. Most Americans these days probably **(2)** _____ (believe) that fewer, not more, people read regularly. One of the reasons for this belief in declining reading habits **(3)** _____ (be) the explosion of the amount of television available. Cable TV subscribers in an area like New York City **(4)** _____ (receive) more than 100 channels.

Another piece of evidence that Americans read less **(5)** _____ (be) the well-documented fall in U.S. student test scores, particularly in comparison to student scores in other countries, such as Japan. However, some studies of student time use **(6)** _____ (have) shown that average Japanese students actually watch *more* TV than their American counterparts. Their success in part **(7)** _____ (come) from also doing more homework than American students.

Some prominent writers such as Camile Paglia **(8)** _____ (have) argued that reading books **(9)** _____ (be) an outdated skill in this age of electronic media. Media critic Neil Postman, on the other hand, **(10)** _____ (have) argued that reading books **(11)** _____ (remain) a uniquely rewarding and necessary activity.

A quick look at their books **(12)** _____ (leave) one a little confused. Paglia's *Sexual Personae* **(13)** _____ (be) 736 pages long, while Postman's books **(14)** _____ (have) tended to be less than 200 pages.

First, identify the subject of the sentence and circle its head noun. Next, put brackets around any modifying phrases following the head noun. Finally, fill in the blank with the verb given.

EXAMPLE: The Library of Congress catalog (system,) [which most U.S. libraries use,]
_____classifies_____ (classify) books as either "fiction" or "nonfiction."

The kind of fiction that each person likes to read **(1)** _____ (be) a matter of individual taste. The four most popular writers in the Gallup survey discussed in the textbook **(2)** _____ (write) in a variety of genres.

One thing that most of the favorite books have in common **(3)** _____ (be) their designation as "popular," or mass-market, reading. This designation, which is made frequently by booksellers and reviewers, **(4)** _____ (be) hard to define. Generally speaking, a book that is unpopular with literary critics **(5)** _____ (be) considered "popular." Supposedly, this kind of book, compared to books typically taught in college literature courses, **(6)** _____ (have) less depth of thought.

However, a review of books considered "popular" over the years **(7)** _____ (show) that the designation can change. Charles Dickens, like a number of other Victorian writers, **(8)** _____ (be) enormously popular with readers in his time, yet today his works are studied widely in college literature courses. Even Shakespeare's plays, widely considered the paradigm of thoughtful literature in English, **(9)** _____ (be) listed as "works of diversion" for students in an eighteenth-century catalog at Yale University.

Whatever they are reading, readers inevitably find certain conditions that improve their reading. Some people **(10)** _____ (find) that eyeglasses, as opposed to contact lenses, **(11)** _____ (help) their reading. Others might prefer a special thing, such as a rocking chair or a cup of coffee. It is clear that desire, not any innate abilities, **(12)** _____ (make) an avid reader.

Fill in the blank with a form of the verb given. In some cases you may have to make additional choices in singular/plural noun of adjective agreement.

EXAMPLE: Both *The Night Manager* and *The Spy Who Came in from the Cold*

_____**were**_____ (be) best-sellers by author John le Carré.

Although both Sue Grafton and Elmore Leonard **(1)** _____ (write) mystery novel, **(2)** _____ (his/her/their) styles are quite different.

Despite the fact that neither Ralph Ellison nor Mary Shelley **(3)** _____ (write) more than a few books, both Ellison and Shelley **(4)** _____ (be) regarded as **(5)** _____ (a major writer/major writers). On the other hand, both Danielle Steel and Louis L'Amour **(6)** _____ (have) written numerous best-sellers without being given much critical attention.

Neither Ray Bradbury nor most other science fiction writers **(7)** _____ (appeal) much to Mariko. She says that either nonfiction books, such as histories and biographies, or a realistic fiction writer like James Clavell **(8)** _____ (interest) her.

(9) _____ (have) either Wan-shan or the other Chinese students read *Iron and Silk* yet? Both that book and the movie of the same name **(10)** _____ (tell) the story of Mark Salzman, an American English teacher in China.

(11) _____ (do) either horror novels or a good suspenseful story appeal to you? If so, either Stephen King or V. C. Andrews **(12)** _____ (be) **(13)** _____ (a good choice/good choices) for you.

If neither the espionage novels of John le Carré nor a book like *Red Storm Rising* **(14)** _____ (appeal) to you, neither a writer like Tom Clancy nor books like *Day of the Jackal* **(15)** _____ (be) **(16)** _____ (a good choice/good choices). Both Tom Clancy and Danielle Steel frequently **(17)** _____ (find) **(18)** _____ (his/her/their) **(19)** _____ (book/books) at the top of best-seller lists.

EXERCISE 4 (Focus 4)

Fill in each blank with the present tense form of the verb given. In some cases you will also need to choose a singular or plural form of a given pronoun. The first one has been done for you as an example.

Yassir's ESL class **(1)** _doesn't have_ (not have) a textbook. Instead **(2)** _____ (they/it) **(3)** _____ (use) four novels. This method of teaching **(4)** _____ (be) called "whole-language instruction." In this method, students are required to do large amounts of non-ESL reading and to respond to their reading in journals, which are read in groups. Vocabulary **(5)** _____ (be) improved by students selecting words to learn from the reading.

Right now Yassir's group **(6)** _____ (write) in **(7)** _____ (their/its) journals. The assignment **(8)** _____ (be) for students to write on how they felt about this method. Some people **(9)** _____ (like) it a lot. They feel that the information that **(10)** _____ (come) from additional reading **(11)** _____ (help) them to understand native speakers better. Other people **(12)** _____ (like) the method less; they feel that the homework **(13)** _____ (be) too time-consuming.

Yassir's group **(14)** _____ (have) some good ideas. Research **(15)** _____ (not favor) any single method of language teaching; rather, education—using any method—that **(16)** _____ (interest) students **(17)** _____ (be) the kind that will be successful. The interested **(18)** _____ (tend) to do well, while the disinterested usually **(19)** _____ (do) poorly.

EXERCISE 5 (Focus 5)

Fill in each blank with the appropriate form of the verb in parentheses.

1. Fifty-five miles per hour _____ (be) the speed limit on some unmarked rural roads in the United States.

2. A pair of binoculars _____ (be) necessary equipment for an ornithologist.

3. Geriatrics _____ (be) the medical field concerned with illnesses that afflict the elderly.

4. The diamond-studded glasses stolen from the home of the famous actress Tessa Tang _____ (be) recovered yesterday.

5. Predicting the influence of the stars on people's lives _____ (be) the work of astrologers.

6. Fewer cases of AIDS _____ (be) reported recently in New York.

7. The bends _____ (be) caused by moving too quickly from a high to a low atmospheric pressure.

8. The Azores _____ (be) located west of Portugal.

9. *Hard Times* _____ (be) written by Charles Dickens.

10. Your extra-sharp pair of scissors _____ (be) on the desk by the bookcase.

11. Tongs _____ (be) useful at a barbecue.

12. "Sports", "Travel," and the "Weekly Review" _____ (be) the only sections of the newspaper I had time to read yesterday.

13. Having one flat tire is bad enough but having two _____ be) even worse.

14. What we want _____ (be) safer streets.

15. Before Pheidippides died in Athens from his 22-mile run, he delivered news that _____ (be) pleasing to his generals: the Greeks had won the battle of Marathon.

16. That all children need lots of encouragement _____ (be) obvious.

17. Migraine headaches _____ (be) excruciating.

EXERCISE 6 (*Focus 6*)

Fill in each blank with the correct form of the verb given in parentheses.

Six of the fifteen best-selling hardcover children's books of all time **(1)** _____ (be) written by Dr. Seuss, the pen name of Theodore Geisel.

One-third of the paperback list **(2)** _____ (be) filled with titles by Laura Ingalls Wilder. A lot of her work **(3)** _____ (deal) with pioneer children in the American midwest in the nineteenth century. A number of her books **(4)** _____ (be) the basis for a popular American TV program, "Little House on the Prairie."

Among adults, nearly everything V. C. Andrews wrote **(5)** _____ (have) sold well. Although Andrews's books have been written by another writer since her death, a lot of her audience **(6)** _____ (know) this, and none of them **(7)** _____ (seem) to mind.

His fans quickly buy almost every book Stephen King **(8)** _____ (have) written. Each of his books **(9)** _____ (have) been a best-seller.

Every year, although a number of new information almanacs **(10)** _____ (be) written, the number of *World Almanacs* sold still **(11)** _____ (continue) to climb.

Nora felt that none of the clerk's advice **(12)** _____ (be) particularly useful as she perused the books in the store. None of the books **(13)** _____ (be) what she was looking for for her father. Her father always made sure that everyone in the family **(14)** _____ (have) an interesting book to read. There **(15)** _____ (be) a large number of interesting titles on the bookshelves at home.

Fill in each blank with the correct form of the verb given.

A small but vocal minority **(1)** _____ (have) objected to the inclusion of some well-known books in school libraries. The majority of the complaints **(2)** _____ (have) centered around racial or sexual themes in the books. Although a 90 percent majority of parents surveyed **(3)** _____ (be) opposed to the removal of the problem books, in most cases, the complainants were given a public hearing. Typically, only a minority of the books in question **(4)** _____ (reveal) sustained prejudicial views of the authors. Rather, the offending passages are usually related to prejudiced characters whom the author condemns.

A sizable majority **(5)** _____ (feel) that the right to free speech is more important than the right to be free from offensive speech. Therefore, these kinds of protests are rarely successful. And although they make good news stories, only a tiny minority of school districts—less than 1 percent nationwide—ever **(6)** _____ (face) this problem.

In regard to computer use, a recent survey reports that a surprising majority of people now **(7)** _____ (own) a personal computer. Of those surveyed only a very small minority **(8)** _____ (insist) that computers are more of a nuisance than a boon. The majority of those who own computers—71 percent, in fact— **(9)** _____ (say) their primary use is for personal word processing. Of those who use an on-line service, the vast majority **(10)** _____ (go) on-line everyday.

Jack and Nigel are fishing together. Jack is a very informal person, whereas Nigel is always formal. Fill in the blanks of their conversation with the correct form of *be* according to the formal and informal rules you studied in your textbook. The first one has been done for you as an example.

Nigel: Would you please hand me a soft drink from the cooler?

Jack: (1) _____ There's _____ cola and ginger ale. Which do you want?

_____There's

Nigel: Either of them (2) _____ fine.

Jack: Hold on a second. Neither of the colas (3) _____ cold. And one of the ginger ales is a diet ginger ale. Which do you want?

Nigel: Either the colas or the regular ginger ale (4) _____ fine. Oh, there

(5) _____ some clean drinking cups as well, right?

Jack: Uh, no. There (6) _____ some cups, but none of them

(7) _____ clean. What's wrong with drinking from the can?

Nigel: Neither your dirty hands nor the can (8) _____ free of the sorts of germs that could ruin a perfectly splendid fishing trip.

Jack: Oh, come off it. Either your fussiness or your complaints

(9) _____ going to ruin the trip.

Nigel: You needn't be so rude. Neither you nor I (10) _____ here to do anything but enjoy ourselves.

Jack: Which, I might add, neither you nor I (11) _____ doing as long as we're arguing instead of fishing.

TOEFL®

Test Preparation Exercises
Units 1–3

Choose the one word or phrase that best completes each sentence.

1. Ngyyet said that neither her mother nor her brothers _____ come with her to the picnic.
   - (A) plan to
   - (B) is planning to
   - (C) plans to
   - (D) has plans to

2. Every one of the workers _____ with the new agreement.
   - (A) is pleased
   - (B) are pleased
   - (C) have been pleased
   - (D) were pleased

3. It seemed so nice when we looked at it in June. The carpet _____ installed and the windows overlooked the park.
   - (A) has just been
   - (B) had just been
   - (C) is just
   - (D) will have just been

4. An overwhelming majority _____ the president's plan.
   - (A) does not support
   - (B) are not going to support
   - (C) do not support
   - (D) were not in support of

5. Angela usually works in the marketing division, but she _____ in sales until Melissa gets out of the hospital.
   - (A) works
   - (B) has worked
   - (C) worked
   - (D) is working

6. Two-thirds of what the candidate said _____ true.
   - (A) were
   - (B) was
   - (C) are
   - (D) seem

7. When the fight broke out, David _____ to Grace.
   - (A) talked
   - (B) will speak with
   - (C) has been talking
   - (D) was talking

8. Counting today, Maria _____ absent from class for four consecutive days.
   - (A) is
   - (B) was
   - (C) has been
   - (D) will be

9. As a result of better engineering, fatalities from car accidents _____ for the past ten years.
   - (A) are declining
   - (B) have declined
   - (C) decline
   - (D) were declining

10. We will not renew our lease in August. Instead, we _____ a house with some friends.
      (A) rent   (C) can rent
      (B) will rent   (D) planned to rent

11. The committee _____ with the project for weeks before the chairman cut their funding.
      (A) had been struggling   (C) struggles
      (B) has been struggling   (D) has struggled

12. Our new apartment is awful. The heater doesn't work, the sink leaks, and the refrigerator _____ a loud noise every time it comes on.
      (A) will make   (C) makes
      (B) has made   (D) made

13. In my essay, I said that the main reason I came to this college _____ its excellent research facilities.
      (A) are   (C) was
      (B) have been   (D) were

14. By the year 2020, world population _____ to 8.2 billion people.
      (A) increases   (C) has increased
      (B) will have increased   (D) increased

15. The binoculars I received for Christmas _____ excellent for birdwatching.
      (A) am   (C) are
      (B) is   (D) was

Identify the *one* underlined word or phrase that must be changed for the sentence to be grammatically correct.

16. Jefferson High School's principal, not the parents, <u>wants</u> to extend the school year, but
                                             A
the students at the school <u>say</u> that their teachers <u>give</u> enough work already, and they
                   B   **C**
<u>need</u> the summer to recover for the next year.
D

17. Neither the workers nor the owner <u>feel</u> that their present contract <u>is</u> acceptable, so they
                             A   **B**
<u>have decided</u> to hire a negotiator to help them <u>reach</u> an agreement.
   C   **D**

18. At the meeting tonight, the mayor <u>will explain</u> what she <u>wants</u> from the police
                                A   **B**
department, and the police <u>is going</u> to explain everything they <u>have asked</u> the mayor for.
                        C   **D**

19. At a transportation conference we <u>went</u> to, a freight company manager <u>said</u> that eight
                           A   **B**
hours of driving <u>were</u> not enough for his drivers to deliver goods, so they often <u>drove</u>
               C   **D**
illegal overtime hours.

20. One of the teachers <u>complained</u> that more than three-fourths of her preparation time

                                                   A

<u>were</u> spent on evaluation, while she <u>felt</u> that she <u>needed</u> more time to prepare lectures

B   **C**   **D**

and class activities.

21. After Marsha <u>was injured</u> in the game, the coach <u>said</u> that although he hoped that her

                         A   **B**

health <u>were</u> going to improve, he <u>was going to</u> remove her from the team so that another

       C   **D**

player could have a chance.

22. My brother-in-law recently <u>had bought</u> a house; he <u>has been studying</u> the mortgage

                                    A   **B**

rates, and <u>feels</u> that now <u>is</u> a good time to buy.

          C   **D**

23. The landlord <u>says</u> he <u>will send</u> someone <u>to fix</u> the heater next week, but we <u>won't</u> believe him.

          A   **B**   **C**   **D**

24. Because <u>he has been feeling</u> tired and <u>wants</u> a change in his life, James <u>has taken</u> a

               A   **B**   **C**

temporary leave of absence from his job and <u>does</u> work with retarded children this summer.

                                           D

25. Shazia <u>is planning</u> to visit Acapulco this winter; her mother just <u>returned</u> from there, and

               A   **B**

<u>had told</u> her how much she <u>enjoyed</u> her vacation.

   C   **D**

26. Jonas <u>is looking</u> at several possible medical schools that he <u>thinks</u> <u>will be</u> good choices

          A   **B**   **C**

for him after he <u>will graduate</u> in May.

              D

27. We <u>were working</u> on our assignment for three hours when a student <u>ran</u> into the lab and

      A   **B**

<u>said</u> that there <u>was</u> a fire.

 C   **D**

28. Mary <u>has written</u> to several publishers about the book that she just <u>finished</u>, and now

      A   **B**

<u>waits</u> to see if any of them <u>will publish</u> it.

 C   **D**

UNIT

Passive Verbs

Underline the passive verb in each sentence below and then explain the most likely reason for its use. In stating your explanations, refer to the following contexts:

A. The focus is on the receiver of an action rather than the performer or agent.

B. The agent is obvious from the context.

C. The agent is unknown.

D. The speaker/writer wishes to avoid mentioning the agent.

1. In Washington yesterday a new law extending maternity and paternity leave was passed. _____

2. Yes, it's true, many things have been neglected around the house lately, but this is going to change. _____

3. In Jane Austen's novel, *Pride and Prejudice*, Mr. Darcy was at first rejected by Elizabeth Bennett. _____

4. Two church windows were cracked in the storm last night. _____

5. Steps are being taken to find the terrorists and bring them to justice. _____

6. Bullfrogs prefer large bodies of water but can be found in bogs and small streams when the ideal conditions are not available. _____

7. If certain genes are damaged, cancer can arise in the organism. _____

8. Science is driven by curiosity. _____

9. This magazine welcomes new contributors. Unsolicited manuscripts, however, will not be returned unless accompanied by an SASE. _____

10. The audience was deeply moved by the performance of the young violinist. _____

Rewrite each sentence below to put the focus on the recipients of the action rather than on the agents of the action. Delete the agent if you do not think it needs to be mentioned.

EXAMPLE: The Olympic Committee included swimming in the first modern Olympic games in 1896.

Swimming was included in the first modern

Olympic games in 1896.

1. The Olympic Committee added diving events in 1904.

2. They clearly mark the swimming pools in competitive swimming.

3. They use antiturbulence lane lines to separate the swimmers and keep the water calm.

4. In fencing, a long wire that passes underneath each fencer's jacket connects the sword tips to lights.

5. A bulb flashes when a fencer makes a hit.

6. People once thought of fungi as plants, but biologists now classify them as a separate kingdom.

7. Legislation has advanced the status of women.

8. Traders are buying and selling stocks in a frenzy of activity today on Wall Street.

9. The next Jupiter space probe will transmit thousands of photographs of the Great Red Spot.

10. Termites were slowly devouring the old Barlow mansion on the hill.

PART A

Underline all the passive verbs in the essay below. The first one has been done for you as an example.

In 1989, more motor vehicles <u>were produced</u> in Japan than in any other country in the world. Although the United States is the world production leader for trucks and buses, 25 percent more passenger cars were manufactured in Japan than in the United States. More vehicles are bought by people in the United States than in any other country, with one car for every 1.3 people. In Japan one car is found for every 4.3 people. In France the ratio is 1 to 2.5, and in Great Britain the ratio is 1 to 3.

Enormous profits are made in automotive manufacturing. In the United States, the first and second largest corporations are car companies (General Motors and Ford), and large portions of the economies of Japan, Germany, France, Italy, Canada, South Korea, and Brazil are devoted to automotive manufacturing. Cars are also manufactured in countries from Argentina to Sweden. In dollar amounts, more automobiles and automotive products are exported from the United States than any other commodity. Yet an even greater number of automobiles and automotive products are imported to the United States.

More people are killed worldwide in auto accidents than by any other type of accidental death. In fact, the rate is more than three times greater than falls, the second-leading cause of accidental death, and greater than the total deaths for falls, drowning, fires, accidental shootings, and poisonings combined. Auto accidents are listed as the eighth leading cause of death in the United States. More lives are lost to auto accidents than to diabetes or AIDS.

There is some good news, though. Since 1970, the fatality rate for auto accidents in the United States has declined 30 percent. This decline was caused mainly by a number of improvements in the design of cars. Nowadays cars in the United States are required to have either air bags or passive restraints, such as automatic seat belts. Energy-absorbing frames are found in most cars, along with reinforced-steel passenger compartments. Some more expensive cars are outfitted with antilock brakes, and most cars carry smaller safety additions such as eye-level rear brakelights and childproof door locks. Since 1970, tougher drunk driving laws have been passed in most states, and mandatory seat belt laws currently exist in 36 states.

One issue related to car safety thought to have had little effect is the general trend toward the manufacture of smaller cars. Over an 11-year period, the best-selling car models have changed from mostly full-sized cars in 1978 to mostly mid-sized and compact cars in 1989. This change is related both to rising gasoline prices and to a decline in consumer confidence in larger American-made cars.

PART B

Separate the passive verbs in the essay above into stative and dynamic passives.

STATIVE PASSIVE	DYNAMIC PASSIVE

Underline the stative passive verb in each of the following sentences and state the use of each, based on the following categories:

> **A.** to describe location or position
>
> **B.** to describe characteristics or qualities
>
> **C.** to describe manner or method
>
> **D.** to describe part-whole relationships
>
> **E.** to describe purpose
>
> **F.** to describe connection
>
> **G.** to describe reputation or association
>
> **H.** to define or name

> EXAMPLE: The nation of Cape Verde <u>is found</u> in the Atlantic Ocean off the west coast of Africa. *(A)*

1. Water is made of two parts hydrogen and one part oxygen.

2. In the British system, liquids of less than a pint are measured in gills.

3. The combination of one part oxygen and two parts deuterium oxide is known as "heavy water."

4. Two-thirds of the earth is covered by water.

5. The molecules of water are connected to each other by a process termed "ionic bonding."

6. A peninsula is surrounded by water on three sides.

7. The sulfuric water found in geysers and hot springs is considered therapeutic.

8. Water turbines are used to produce electricity from dammed water.

9. Fish ladders are designed to allow salmon to swim over dams as they go upstream to spawn.

10. Lakes Huron, Ontario, Michigan, Erie, and Superior, which are collectively termed the Great Lakes, are found in the United States and Canada, and are the largest body of fresh water in the world.

Underline the complex passives in the following passage.

Folk Customs and Lore: Doors to Mysterious Britain

(1) There is always more to a nation than what we read in standard history books or economic surveys. **(2)** Folk customs and lore are especially rich sources of information that give us a certain "feel" for a place, a people, and the past, and restore a sense of wonder generally missing in observations restricted to "the hard facts." **(3)** Britain, because of its antiquity, is fertile ground for study. **(4)** Add to this a certain endearing eccentricity of character and what some would call "a haunted geography" and you have the promise of some intriguing revelations.

(5) Take, for example, the Furry Dance at Helston in Cornwall, held annually on May 8. **(6)** It is reputed to be one of oldest examples of a communal spring festival dance still surviving. **(7)** It is claimed that the dance has been performed without a break—except in times of war and pestilence—since pre-Christian times. **(8)** According to one local legend, however, the dance is said to commemorate the victory of St. Michael the Archangel over the devil in a struggle for possession of the town. **(9)** Today the dancing begins at six in the morning with the town band parading through the streets followed by all the children. **(10)** It is considered appropriate for everyone to participate, and at noon the mayor, wearing his chain of office, leads all the dancing townspeople through all the main streets and into gardens, shops, and houses, in one door and, if possible, out through another, to bring the luck of summer to the owners and tenants and drive out the darkness of winter.

(11) It is known that many customs have vanished since the industrial revolution, including one called "barring-out" the schoolmaster, which was believed to have taken place at varying times during the year and in many parts of Britain. **(12)** On the appointed morning, the children locked the schoolmaster out of his own school and refused to let him in until he had granted a holiday for that day or, according to some of the earliest accounts, promised a number of holidays during the coming months. **(13)** All his attempts to enter were fiercely resisted, and while the siege continued, it is said, the defenders shouted or sang traditional barring-out rhymes.

(14) Every land has its share of ghost and spirit lore, but it is conjectured that Britain is the most haunted of them all. **(15)** Some spirit visitations are relatively benign, others grim. **(16)** It was recently reported that on the grounds of

Holland House in the heart of London, a headless ghost (presumably the first owner's son-in-law, beheaded during the civil war) was seen walking in the moonlight. **(17)** Holland Park, in which the house stands, also has its mysteries, and it is said that people have seen their doubles there. **(18)** (Traditionally, to see one's double warns of death within a year.) **(19)** In Glencoe, in the Scottish Highlands, where a ghastly massacre took place in 1692, many people claim to have felt a brooding presence, a palpable oppression, and to have heard the sounds of sword against shield, faint cries, far-off moans, and calls for vengeance.

(20) It is supposed that belief in the existence of fairies was still strong among the country folk of Britain until quite recently, and there are many stories telling of fairies' subterranean palaces, their hard-working helpfulness, and their love of music, dancing, and mischief. **(21)** Humans were thought to have been lured into fairy lands to be entertained for what seemed a short while, only to find on returning home that a hundred years of our time had passed. **(22)** Stories are common of youths who, having passed a night or two in fairy land, return to find their poor cottages tall mansions, and their lords' castles ivy-clad ruins; the lords, while conversing with great grandchildren, suddenly crumble into heaps of ashes.

(23) Though it is undoubtedly true that many a folk custom has not found its way into actual practice in the twentieth century, many still remain. **(24)** And while we may take a lot of folklore with a grain of salt, it must be admitted that a good tale, full of surprise and mystery, is what we all like to hear.

EXERCISE 6   *(Focus 5)*

For each of the following numbered sentence groups, choose and circle the sentence, (a) or (b), that best fits the context, using the principles of introducing or continuing topics as discussed in Focus 5. Read each numbered group as the beginning of a written article or spoken announcement.

1. It is believed that out of the roughly one hundred billion galaxies within range of our telescopes, each galaxy is home to a hundred billion stars.

   (a) It is surmised that half of these stars have planets.

   (b) Half of these stars are surmised to have planets.

2. **(a)** After many years as king of Athens, the ancient Greek hero Theseus was said to have lost the favor of his people and to have been forced to leave the city.

   (b) It is said that after many years as king of Athens, the ancient Greek hero Theseus lost the favor of his people and was forced to leave the city. He retired to the court of Lycomedes, the king of Scyros, who at first received him kindly, but afterwards treacherously slew him.

3. (a) It was reported today that the space shuttle Discovery nearly lost power as it came in for a landing.

(b) The space shuttle Discovery was reported to have nearly lost power today as it came in for a landing. A malfunctioning fuse was thought to be responsible.

4. In India, it is considered dangerous to travel on either a Tuesday or a Saturday.

(a) It is thought that the gods to whom those days are dedicated are tricksters quite capable of playing pranks on vulnerable humans.

(b) The gods to whom those days are dedicated are thought to be tricksters quite capable of playing pranks on vulnerable humans.

EXERCISE 7 (Focus 5)

The columns below have information about old British superstitions related to animals. Match the descriptions in the first column to the results in the second column to form superstitions. Express each situation and result in sentences with two complex sentence structures: a *that* clause complex passive and an infinitive clause.

EXAMPLE: It was believed that if you saw a hare at the outset of a journey, the journey would not go well.

OR

Seeing a hare at the outset of a journey was believed to to be a sign that the journey would not go well.

ACTION/CONDITION	RESULT
1. if a toad crossed your path	a. you would have a long life
2. if a cat sneezed	b. bad luck would come to you
3. if a lizard crossed the path of a bridal procession	c. a death would be imminent
4. if you saw a golden butterfly at a funeral	d. you would have good luck
5. if a weasel squealed	e. a legacy would come your way
6. if a beetle crawled out of your shoe	f. your children would do well in school
7. if a spider fell on you from the ceiling of a house	g. the marriage would have problems
8. if you fed horsehair to your children	h. it would rain

HINTS: Spiders, butterflies, and toads had positive associations.
Beetles, lizards and especially weasels had negative associations.
Cats were associated with weather.

1. _____

2. _____

3. _____

4. _____

5. _____

6. _____

7. _____

8. _____

EXERCISE 8   (Focus 6)

Imagine that you are a journalist being interviewed by a panel of students. The following are questions you have been asked about past, current, and future events. Give a response to each question by making a complex passive statement from the information in brackets. Include an agent only if you think it is necessary. Use one of the following verbs: *expect, rumor, believe, assume, allege.*

EXAMPLE: **Q:** Why did they stop construction of the Black River nuclear power plant? [Inspectors thought the foundation was faulty]

A: *The foundation was believed to be faulty.*

OR

It was believed that the foundation was faulty.

1. Why is the senator from Kansas vacationing in New Hampshire? [The consensus is he will run in the primary elections.]

   _____

2. Why has Congressman Loren not been seen for two weeks? [Word has it that he is undergoing treatment in a clinic in Arizona.]

   _____

3. Why did the Rodax company take their new painkiller off the market? [They think the results of the lab tests were misinterpreted.]

   _____

4. Why haven't we heard any more news about the Fisher case? [Most people guess it was settled out of court.]

   _____

5. What's the latest update about the fire that burned down the Surf Hotel? [Police think it was the work of arsonists.]

   _____

6. Is it true that we'll be seeing some new faces on the White House staff? [Our sources have it that there will be an announcement shortly about a major reshuffling.]

   _____

    Here are some additional facts from the *World Almanac* and purported facts from "Harper's Index" (*Harper's* magazine) and "Facts Out of Context" (*In Context, A Quarterly of Humane Sustainable Culture*). Information considered to be a fact is indicated by (F); information thought to be possibly true is indicated by (?). Your task is to rewrite the following information in complete sentences. Use the past participle of the verb given in parentheses.

EXAMPLE: (?) Number of children admitted to hospital emergency rooms last year for injuries involving shopping carts: 32,866 (report)

It is reported that the number of children admitted to hospital emergency rooms last year for injuries involving shopping carts was 32,866.

OR

The number of children admitted to hospital emergency rooms last year for injuries involving shopping carts is reported to have been 32,866.

1. (?) There are approximately 75,000 edible plants found in nature (think)

2. (?) Estimated number of birds that are killed in collisions with TV broadcast towers each year: 1,250,000 (estimate)

3. (F) Highest mountain in South America: Aconcagua, Argentina (know)

4. (?) Estimated number of unsolicited phone calls made by U.S. telemarketers each second: 200 (believe)

5. (?) Amount of time required to set the table for a banquet at London's Buckingham Palace: three days (speculate)

6. (?) Maximum fine for parking illegally overnight in Tokyo: $1,400 (report)

_____

_____

7. (?) Earth's population around 8,000 B.C., when farmers began harvesting domesticated plants: 4 million (believe)

_____

_____

8. (?) Number of people born every 10 days in 1991: 4 million (say)

_____

_____

EXERCISE 10 **(Focus 7)**

Circle the passive verbs in the following passages. Then explain why each passive is used.

1. These pets don't sting, they don't bark, and they won't replace hats. Still the iguana is becoming fashionable in New York City. This summer, the iguanas, their nails cut to avoid scratching, could be seen perched on the heads or shoulders of their owners. When they were taken outside, usually when the weather was warm, many owners used harnesses.

   (From the _New York Times_, Sunday, September 1, 1996.)

   _____

2. The most relentless borrowers of English words have been the Japanese. The number of English words currently used in Japanese has been estimated to be as high as 20,000.

   _____

3. Chinese writing possesses one great advantage over other languages: It can be read everywhere. Chinese is not really a language at all, but more a family of loosely related dialects. In some places one dialect is spoken over a very wide area, but in other parts of the country, particularly in the deep south, the dialects can change every two or three miles.

   _____

4. According to a Gallup poll, the crossword is the most popular sedentary recreation, occupying thirty million Americans for part of every day. The very first crossword, containing just thirty-two clues, appeared in the New York *World* on December 21, 1913. It had been thought up as a space filler by an expatriate Englishman named Arthur Wynne. It wasn't until 1924, when Simon & Schuster brought out a volume of crossword puzzles priced at $1.35, that it became a hit. By the end of the year, a half a million copies had been sold, and crossword puzzles were a craze across America.

(Nos. 2, 3 and 4 adapted from Bill Bryson, *The Mother Tongue*. New York: William Morrow, 1990.)

EXERCISE 11 (*Focus 7*)

After each sentence or group of sentences below, add a sentence with a passive verb to create cohesion, using the information given in parentheses.

1. William Harvey discovered the circulation of the blood. (Before the publication of Harvey's work in 1628, people did not recognize the role of the heart in circulation.)

   _____

   _____

2. After carbohydrates and proteins, lipids make up the third most important class of the molecules of life. (Carbon, hydrogen, and oxygen build lipids.)

   _____

   _____

3. Mars is only half the size of the earth. Its "year" is two earth-years long and we can tell that it has seasons because we can watch the polar caps wax and wane. (Not water but frozen carbon dioxide makes up the polar caps of Mars.)

   _____

   _____

4. Early in its history, the earth had craters like those on the moon. (Since that time, however, the forces of erosion and weathering have destroyed almost all of the early craters.)

   _____

   _____

5. The phylum cyanobacteria includes single-celled organisms that float on the surface of water. (We refer to them loosely as "blue-green algae." People believe that they were the first living things on earth.)

_____

_____

6. Like the earth, the sun has a magnetic field. (Scientists think this field reverses itself every eleven years.)

_____

_____

(Adapted from James Trefil, 1001 _Things Everyone Should Know about Science._ New York: Doubleday, 1992.)

UNIT
5 Article Usage

(Focus 1)

Fill in each blank with *a/an*, *the*, or Ø.

The caravan entered between two ranks of guards. **(1)** _____ traders continued on to **(2)** _____ market, while **(3)** _____ guide took me to **(4)** _____ inn of the foreigners. **(5)** _____ guide made **(6)** _____ camel kneel down in front of **(7)** _____ large pavilion like **(8)** _____ barracks. When he carried my traveling bags inside, I realized that it was **(9)** _____ inn. It was divided into two wings separated by **(10)** _____ extended reception hall; each wing contained **(11)** _____ adjoining rooms whose sides were constructed of **(12)** _____ hair cloth. **(13)** _____ room chosen for me was simple, even primitive; its floor was sandy, and it possessed **(14)** _____ bed (which consisted of **(15)** _____ wooden board laid on **(16)** _____ ground), **(17)** _____ chest for clothes, and **(18)** _____ cushions in **(19)** _____ middle. No sooner had I finished checking through my bags than I hurried to bed with **(20)** _____ eagerness of someone deprived of **(21)** _____ normal sleep for **(22)** _____ full month. I slept deeply until woken by **(23)** _____ day's heat. As though unwell, I rose from my bed and passed through into **(24)** _____ reception hall, which was crammed with **(25)** _____ guests, all of whom were seated in front of their rooms having **(26)** _____ breakfast. **(27)** _____ short man, slightly stout, wearing only **(28)** _____ loincloth, came up to me. "I am Fam, **(29)** _____ owner of **(30)** _____ inn," he said smiling. "Did you have **(31)** _____ good night?"

(From Naguib Mahfouz, *The Journey of Ibn Fattouma* [trans. Denys Johnson-Davies]. New York: Doubleday, 1992.)

Fill in each blank with *a/an*, *the*, or Ø. Indicate whether the noun is classified or identified by writing either <u>C</u> for classified or <u>I</u> for identified above it.

                       I   C

EXAMPLE: **The** earliest road vehicle powered by **an** engine was built in 1770.

1. Ali is learning to fly _____ plane.

2. _____ water in _____ well is filled with _____ algae. You shouldn't drink it unless it's been filtered first.

3. _____ mountains of Austria are some of the most picturesque in the world.

4. "Oh, no, I hate _____ peas and _____ carrots," cried the little girl when she looked at _____ vegetables on _____ table.

5. Author Paul Theroux is famous for taking _____ trains all over the world.

6. _____ global economy is dependent on _____ oil.

7. I wish everybody would ride _____ bicycles and leave their cars at home.

8. _____ sheep in _____ field were marked with red dye.

9. _____ government was accused of _____ corruption.

10. I heard _____ shot ring out through _____ forest.

Answer the following questions with noun phrases. Use *a/an*, *the*, or Ø to show that the noun is classified or identified.

EXAMPLE: What kind of person is successful?

    A person who is happy _____ (classified)

  What feature of television don't you like?

    The commercials _____ (identified)

1. What kind of animal makes the best pet?

_____

2. What feature of English do you find especially difficult?

_____

3. What type of book do you enjoy reading?

_____

4. What feature of computers do you appreciate?

_____

5. What part of work do you dislike?

_____

Choose the correct article before each noun phrase and then refer to the explanations below to explain your choices.

A. *The* is used with unique nouns.

B. *The* is used before superlatives.

C. *The* is used before ordinals.

D. *The* is used before modifiers which make the noun that follows specific.

E. *The* is used in phrases that refer to a specific part of a whole group.

F. *The* is used with identifiable nouns followed by a modifying *of*-phrase.

G. *The* is used before adjectives that represent groups of people.

H. *The* is used with certain nouns as a general example of something.

I. *The* is used before locations associated with typical or habitual activities.

J. *The* is used with a noun that has been identified in some way.

K. *A/an* or Ø is used to indicate a type, group, or class.

EXAMPLE: (A/<u>The</u>) only reason that band is popular is because of (a/<u>the</u>) strange videos it produces.

[The only reason—**D**; the strange videos—**J**]

1. We bid on (a/the) second item in (a/the) auction. _____

2. Barbara doesn't ride (a/the) subway late at night unless she's with (a/the/ Ø) friends. _____

3. (A/The) end of (a/the) play was very stirring. _____

4. (A/The) moon was half full but still provided enough light for us to see (a/the) trail. _____

5. Both of (a/the) candidates are promising tax cuts to (a/the/Ø) rich. _____

6. (A/The) most challenging assignment I ever had was (a/the) physics project. _____

7. A lot of teenagers like to hang out at (a/the) mall. _____

8. Lots of paperwork waits in (a/the) in-basket in front of me. Reluctant to move toward (a/the) pile of forms, I stare out (a/the) window for (a/the) fiftieth time this drab Monday morning. _____

9. (A/The) function of (a/the) machine was not apparent at first. _____

10. Seventy percent of (a/the) population of Sudan is illiterate. _____

11. (A/The) main reason we went to (a/the) lecture was to get a look at (a/the) most famous living poet. _____

12. For (a/the) ignorant (a/the) state of bliss is no longer guaranteed. _____

Find and correct the errors in the following sentences.

EXAMPLE: The drug dealer was sentenced to twenty years in ~~the~~ jail.

1. We need to speak with total honesty to each other. It's time for a heart to a heart talk.

2. Laura's favorite meal is a breakfast.

3. They said they would let us know by the phone.

4. The time is the money.

5. I don't like to study during day.

6. The heart attack victim was declared dead on the arrival at the hospital.

7. We regretted that we didn't take the heed of the old man's warning about not crossing the desert at night.

8. After the rescue team pulled the drowning child from the water, one of them performed mouth to the mouth resuscitation.

9. The only way we could cross the river was on a horseback.

10. Catholics are obliged to go to the church on Sundays.

For each of the following pairs of sentences check the option that makes a general rather than a particular reference about the italicized noun phrase.

EXAMPLE: **(a)** *Plants* make their food by photosynthesis. ✔

    (b) Mara's house is filled with *plants*.

1. **(a)** A *sinus problem* can be the result of an allergy.

   (b) David developed *a sinus problem* when he moved to California.

2. **(a)** *The mouse* on my desk has a sleek new design.

   (b) *The mouse* is a peripheral device used with a computer.

3. **(a)** A *cure* for AIDS has been elusive.

   (b) The physician thought that chemotherapy might be *a cure* for the patient's cancer.

4. **(a)** Some *rollercoasters* have been declared national historical sites.

   (b) *Rollercoasters* provide thrills for thousands of people in amusement parks around the world.

5. **(a)** *The tripod* is particularly useful to nature photographers who want to capture detail.

   (b) *The tripod* I bought recently has a quick-release mechanism.

6. **(a)** *The telephone* has changed a lot in the last twenty-five years.

   (b) *The telephone* I ordered has a built-in answering machine.

7. **(a)** *Poetry* may have originally been sung or chanted.

   (b) Café Nuovo will present an evening of *poetry* starting at 7.

8. **(a)** We explored *caves* in Borneo.

   (b) *Caves* commonly form in areas of limestone.

9. **(a)** A *tree* can be either coniferous or deciduous.

   (b) A *tree* that everyone loves in the fall is the sugar maple.

10. **(a)** *The octopus* is a mollusk, just as the snail is.

    (b) *The octopus* squirted a stream of ink at the shark.

EXERCISE 7 *(Focus 6)*

Some of the sentences below contain mistakes in usage of abstract generic *the*. Explain the mistakes and correct them.

EXAMPLE: The eraser is used to remove pencil marks.

(*Eraser* is a simple inanimate object.)

Correction: _____ An eraser _____

OR

_____ Erasers are used to remove pencil marks. _____

1. The cheese is made from milk.

_____

2. The light bulb was invented by Thomas Edison.

_____

3. The blue whale is the largest mammal in the world.

_____

4. The left-handed people die on average earlier than others.

_____

5. The diamond is the hardest stone.

_____

6. The hydrogen is the first element on the atomic table.

_____

7. The nectarine is a cross between the peach and the apricot.

_____

8. The tie is worn by many executives throughout the world.

_____

9. The Arabian horses are prized for their speed and beauty.

_____

EXERCISE 8 (Focus 7)

Match each of the groups below with a suitable generalization and write a complete sentence with the information. Indicate optional use of _the_ by putting it in parentheses. The first one has been done as an example.

1. redwood	**a.** had a vast empire in the nineteenth century
2. Swiss	**b.** also known as sequoias
3. backpacker	**c.** believe in reincarnation
4. smoker	**d.** live in the Four Corners region of the United States
5. Hindu	**e.** tend to be thin and wiry
6. British	**f.** believe they are being discriminated against
7. marathon runner	**g.** are the largest group of insects
8. socialist	**h.** noted for their banks and their mountain scenery
9. Navajo	**i.** must possess excellent mathematical skills
10. jazz musician	**j.** advocate free universal medical coverage
11. beetle	**k.** value light-weight equipment
12. computer programmer	**l.** like to improvise

1. _____ (The) redwoods are also known as sequoias. _____

2. _____

3. _____

4. _____

5. _____

6. _____

7. _____

8. _____

9. _____

10. _____

11. _____

12. _____

(Focus 8)

Some of the following sentences contain mistakes in usage of the article *a(n)* to describe a generalized instance of something. Correct the sentences that are wrong.

EXAMPLE: A tongue is the strongest muscle in the body. _The tongue_

1. A cheetah is the world's fastest land animal. _____

2. A seismologist studies the factors that produce earthquakes. _____

3. A photovoltaic cell is the heart of all modern electronics. _____

4. A compact disc was invented by RCA. _____

5. A sirocco is a hot wind in the Mediterranean region that blows from the east. _____

6. A professor in a university is usually required to have a Ph.D. _____

7. A liver is responsible for cleaning blood. _____

8. A potato is native to the Americas. _____

9. A computer makes editing one's mistakes much easier. _____

10. A stomach digests food. _____

EXERCISE 10   **(Focus 9)**

Fill in each blank with a word of your own choosing plus an article, where necessary.

EXAMPLE: _____ A sail _____ is a piece of material used to catch the wind and move a boat forward.

1. _____ is a black-and-white striped horse-like animal found in Africa.

2. _____ are instruments used by astronomers to study the stars.

3. _____ is a tool used to pound in and remove nails.

4. _____ are medical personnel who fix teeth.

5. _____ is a sport played with nine players, a bat, and a ball.

6. _____ is an insect that begins life as a caterpillar before it acquires its beautiful wings.

7. _____ is water that has frozen.

8. _____ is a sweet, chewable substance made from chicle and sold under names such as Chiclets, Doublemint, and Juicy Fruit.

9. _____ is a household implement used to sweep floors.

10. _____ are lenses worn to overcome defects in vision.

Fill in each blank with the correct body part and an article where necessary, and choose the correct form of the verb given.

EXAMPLE: ___The navel___ (is/are) the scar left on the stomach from the removal of the umbilical cord.

1. _____ (pump/pumps) blood throughout the body.

2. _____ (cover/covers) the outside of the body.

3. _____ (filter/ filters) waste from the bloodstream.

4. _____ (is/are) used to hear.

5. _____ (is/are) used to speak and eat.

6. _____ (is/are) skin covering the head.

7. _____ (is/are) enlarged through exercise.

8. _____ (enable/enables) humans to think.

9. _____ (is/are) used in breathing.

10. _____ (is/are) used to smell.

Fill in each blank with the names of an illness given below, the appropriate article where necessary, and the correct form of be.

EXAMPLE: ___Arthritis___ (is/are) a disease that primarily affects the joints.

| leprosy | rabies | heart attack | AIDS | fracture |
| flu | cholera | ulcer | cold | mumps |

1. _____ (is/are) spread primarily by animal bites.

2. _____ (is/are) a common winter illness that produces mild body aches and a runny nose.

3. _____ (is/are) the popular name for an illness that is similar to the common cold but is more severe and is caused by several types of viruses.

4. _____ (is/are) a fatal, incurable disease transmitted primarily through sexual contact and the use of contaminated IV needles.

5. _____ (is/are) a sudden occurrence of heart failure.

6. _____ (is/are) an open sore, often found in the stomach and produced by stress.

7. _____ (is/are) an intestinal disease that produces a high fever and is often contracted by eating contaminated seafood.

8. _____ (is/are) a communicable disease characterized by swelling of the salivary glands.

9. _____ (is/are) is a disfiguring infectious disease of the skin and nerves characterized by lesions, white scabs, and deformities.

10. _____ (is/are) a break in a bone.

6 Reference Words and Phrases

EXERCISE 1 (*Focus 1*)

Complete the crossword puzzle with the appropriate reference forms.

ACROSS

1. I had a very hard time with chemistry. _____ was too difficult for me.
3. John and Richard never get tired of visiting England. They find the _____ charming and delightful.
5. The conference will concern alternative forms of energy. _____ will be examined in detail.
7. Rita called last night to tell me Brenda got arrested. I still can't believe _____.

DOWN

2. The man got angry, started shouting, threatening, and waving his fist. _____ responses were completely inappropriate.
4. We scanned the horizon through a pair of binoculars to try to see the mountains. Unfortunately, the clouds were so thick that we couldn't see _____ at all.
5. Have you ever made crêpes? _____ are easy to prepare.
6. Lots of children today do not see very much of their parents. They also spend vast amounts of time watching TV. _____ conditions are hardly conducive to a healthy society.
7. Paul claims that the voting age should be lowered to sixteen. I can't agree with _____ at all.

Keeping in mind the referents in brackets, fill in each blank with *the* + a noun phrase or a demonstrative adjective + a noun phrase. The type of reference you should use—repetition of the entire referent, partial repetition, classification of referent, synonym, or paraphrase—is given in parentheses.

EXAMPLE: Most languages show some [gender-based differences].

_These differences_____ may show up in a variety of contexts. (partial repetition)

1. [Sex-based differences] are found not just in tone and voice characteristics, but in the way the language itself is written. In English, _____ are found in the names of occupations and roles. (partial repetition)

2. A number of [occupations and role names for men become derogatory] in their feminine forms. _____ has resulted in lessened or modified usage of the feminine forms of many word pairs such as major/majorette, star/starlet, master/mistress, and governor/governess. (paraphrase)

3. [Men's names] are frequently modified for women, but the reverse rarely happens. _____ such as Robert, George, Louis, and Paul have feminine counterparts (Roberta, Georgette, Louise, and Paulette), but there are no male names for Elizabeth, Laura, Jane, or Katherine. (repetition of entire referent)

4. Women's names are often given [the suffix *-ie* or *-y*.] _____ is found far less frequently in male names: Judy, Kathy, Patty, Tracy, Terry, and Betty are common adult women's names, but Billy, Jimmy, Robbie, and Johnny are more often associated with boys than with men. (classification of referent)

5. In Japan, women also are traditionally given names with [the suffix *-ko*.] _____ is the written character for "child," and is found in the common names Masako, Takako, Hiroko, and Keiko. (partial repetition)

6. Wives in English-speaking countries [have traditionally adopted their husband's names] but never the opposite—Mrs. John Smith, but never Mr. Mary Smith. _____ is changing, however. (paraphrase)

7. There are also a number of [derogatory terms] for females that have no male equivalent. _____, such as *divorcée*, are almost exclusively applied to women. (synonym)

8. A more subtle problem concerns [words] that have no overt sexual specification, but become sexist in some contexts. _____ signifying hair color, for example, are gender-neutral as adjectives ("my brother has blonde hair"), but tend to signify females when used as nouns ("a brunette moved in next door"). (repetition of entire referent)

9. Another [problem] is caused by the use of masculine pronouns for universal reference ("each student needs to bring his own pencil"). _____ is caused by the lack of a gender-neutral third-person singular pronoun in English. (repetition of entire referent)

10. Offices and institutions often try to avoid sexist language with [guidelines] for nonsexist usage. However, _____ multiply so quickly that people tend to resort to what they began with—their own best judgment. (synonym)

EXERCISE 3 (Focus 2)

Make up a sentence with a *the* reference or demonstrative reference to follow and elaborate each of the sentences below. The referent is underlined. Try to use a variety of reference types.

EXAMPLE: The finest friends never hesitate when you ask for their help.

These friends will come to your aid day or night. or

They will come to your aid day or night.

1. According to the great philosophers, generosity is the sign of a wise person.

   _____

   _____

2. The abilities to concentrate completely on what another is saying and to understand the emotions behind the words are critically important for good communication.

   _____

   _____

3. A recent study has shown there is a link between generosity and efficiency in the way organizations work.

   _____

   _____

4. Is there really a way to take the savagery out of drive, ambition, power, and pride?

   _____

   _____

5. Redefining excellence and achievement is a large part of the work of the next century.

   _____

   _____

   _____

EXERCISE 4 (Focus 3)

Decide whether *it, they, them,* or *the* + a noun phrase is appropriate for each blank. If *the* + a noun phrase should be used, choose a noun phrase that fits the context. More than one answer may be possible.

EXAMPLE: Angel and Luis both finished the season with twenty goals apiece. **The players** _____ tied for the league scoring championship. (*They* is also possible.)

1. **Javier:** I read that women tend to smile more when they speak.
   Beatrice: Don't believe _____! I know plenty of women, such as my boss, who *never* smile.

2. Pat is working on a thesis dealing with the difficulties of nonnative English speakers learning final *s*. She should finish _____ by July.

3. The survey found that students in general were pleased with the college, but would like to have more classes scheduled on nights and weekends, extended library hours, and better food in the cafeteria. _____ will be discussed at the next meeting of the college council.

4. The Bulls and the Suns played a tremendous game. However, _____ prevailed in the final minutes and won by a point.

5. Sue is trying to decide whether to buy a Ford, a Dodge, or a Honda. All of _____ are attractive in some way.

6. Going to a Shakespeare play can be a real challenge because of the rich language and obscure allusion. Some of **(a)** _____ may be archaic, and references are frequently unknown to people who haven't previously studied **(b)** _____.

7. The silk melons need to be fertilized every week, but the snow peas only need regular watering. While I'm gone, then, be sure to add some fertilizer when you water _____.

8. The doctors found that the mysterious illness was hereditary, passed on through the father, yet could be treated with changes in lifestyle and minor drug treatment. _____ were published in a medical journal.

9. Pasta and seafood seem to make up most of the entrées on the menu. Luckily for us, _____ are our favorite things to eat.

10. John said he had to abandon his solo hike in the mountains because of being bothered by flying saucers. Can you believe _____?

EXERCISE 5 (Focus 4)

Put an appropriate demonstrative form in each blank: *this, that, these,* or *those*. If you think more than one might be appropriate, discuss in class the contexts (including speaker attitude) in which each might be used.

1. **Tara:** After I finish work on **(a)** _____ project, I'll be free to help you.

   John: But you've been working on **(b)** _____ project for months! Aren't you ever going to finish?

2. I do not agree with _____ people who oppose the council's recommendations.

3. After leaving her country to live in Italy for a year, Nelly moved to Germany and then Canada before she settled here. _____ is why she entered college a few years later than she wanted.

4. Who made _____ muddy tracks on my clean carpet?

5. I heard that Pham had spoken in favor of the nominee. _____ made everyone confident that she must be good.

6. The median age for first marriages in the United States has risen by 15 percent over the last thirty years. During that same period, the divorce rate has more than doubled. _____ statistics lead one to expect that the birth rate has also declined—down 30 percent at the same time.

7. Ken, I'm asking you to look carefully at my plan. _____ is the best hope we have for getting the company out of debt.

8. You should beware of _____ schemes in which you are offered a free vacation if you will only agree to come listen to a sales presentation for condominiums.

9. Chapter 1 gave an overview of the nervous system. It gave descriptions and diagrams of the neuron, the brain, and the spinal cord. It showed the main nerves of the body, and explained how sensory charges were translated from electrical impulses into sensations. _____ chapter also gave a basic description of the main areas of the brain.

10. If we make our airline reservations immediately, we can save 50 percent. _____ seems like a great deal.

EXERCISE 6 (Focus 5)

For the following contexts, use a demonstrative adjective and a classifying or descriptive noun to refer to the information in brackets.

EXAMPLE: Cats are [fast, agile, strong, smart, and well-camouflaged.]

__These traits_____ have made them formidable hunters.

1. Cats have [extremely sharp teeth]. _____ makes it easy for them to devour their prey quickly.

2. The candidate said he would [increase jobs, lower taxes, defeat crime, and make college affordable for everyone]. _____ have excited some people, but made others skeptical.

3. Certain cynics have claimed that [greed and self-centeredness] are important for motivation. If unchecked, however, _____ can lead to the destruction of society.

4. ["Vanish into thin air," "play fast and loose," "be tongue-tied," "make a virtue of necessity"]—_____ are among hundreds coined by Shakespeare.

5. I've always liked [to stay up late at night and sleep until late in the morning]. _____ would get me nowhere, my mother always warned.

6. [Impression: Sunrise, Haystack in Field, Dawn on the Seine, and Waterlilies] are a sampling of what is now on display at the National Gallery of Art. _____ by Claude Monet will remain on exhibit until the end of the month.

7. If you want to expand your vocabulary, [you should read for at least an hour every day]. _____ will give you a better command of the language.

8. Early morning and late afternoon is [when the light is low and the colors are richest]. _____ provide photographers with the best opportunities for getting excellent shots.

9. [Carry travelers' checks; don't keep your wallet in your back pocket; make sure your hotel door is securely locked; don't drink the tap water unless you know that it's been purified]. _____ will insure that you have a safe trip.

10. She said she was late because [her car broke down and her dog was sick]. None of us in the office found that _____ were very convincing.

EXERCISE 7 (Focus 6)

Put an appropriate reference form in each blank, following the instructions in parentheses when given. The referent is in brackets. Use one of the following forms: (1) *it*; (2) *the* + noun phrase; (3) demonstrative adjective *this, that, these,* or *those* + noun phrase; or (4) demonstrative pronoun *this, that, these,* or *those*. For some blanks more than one choice might be possible.

EXAMPLE: They're predicting hail over the weekend. _____**This**_____ is going to damage the crops if they're not protected. (Also possible: ___**The hail**___)

1. Did you watch [the game] last night? I've seen a lot of championship games, but _____ was the best ever. (emphasize the referent)

2. **Linda:** Have you heard that [the writing lab is going to get new computers]?

    Pat: Yes, Dr. Wells told me about _____. (put less emphasis on the referent)

3. In the summer semester, classes meet at much closer intervals, so [there is much less time to complete assignments]. _____ is why you should carefully consider the type of class you take in the summer.

4. We're planning [to visit St. Paul's] the same day we go to Covent Garden, but we're not sure if there will be time for _____. (emphasize the referent)

5. [The book I'm reading now] is pretty boring, but you should read the one I read before _____. (put less emphasis on the referent)

6. **Jeff:** Did you know that [we always see the same side of the moon]?

    Amy: Be serious! Everyone knows _____.

7. What [a magnificent dinner]! _____ is the best meal you've ever cooked!

8. [This homework problem] kept me up until two o'clock last night. Do you know how to solve _____?

9. **Lia:** Have you heard that the school is going to build a stadium and start up a football team?

    Reza: No, I hadn't heard _____.

10. [The judge fined the defendant $2,000] for lighting a cigarette in a non-smoking restaurant. Everyone thought that _____ was excessive. (emphasize the referent)

Put an appropriate reference form in each blank.

Several environmentalists were asked what the average citizen could do to help preserve and protect the diversity of life on the planet. Here is how one of _____ responded to _____.

"First, you must know and love your area. Get outdoors and experience _____. Carry along field guides and learn the plants and animals, not only their names but their life histories and ecological relationships. As you become intimately involved with _____ and their habitats—the forests, grasslands, rivers, lakes, marshes, deserts, and seashores—you cannot help but love _____. And what you love you will want to protect.

"But in protecting local areas, it is essential to keep the big picture in mind. Talk with scientists and professional conservationists to find out which of _____ you know locally are in greatest need of conservation—for example, _____ that are found nowhere else and have declined greatly or _____ that are at great risk. Then work with conservation groups and other citizens to get _____ protected. _____ can be done!"

(Reed N. Ross, quoted in "Ten Things (At Least) You Can Do To Save Life's Diversity," compiled by William Stolzenburg, *Nature Conservancy*, July/August 1996, p. 18.)

Fill in each blank with the appropriate reference using *such*.

EXAMPLE: The doctor said that Lisa needed to eat more spinach, kale, broccoli, and green beans while she was pregnant. __*Such vegetables*__ are high in the kinds of vitamins that her baby needs.

1. The social services board planned, among other things, to open another shelter and expand its present job training service. _____ were intended to reduce the number of homeless people in the city.

2. The store was always filled with customers, but every day it seemed there were more unexpected bills coming in—a leaky roof that had to be fixed, an increase in fire insurance premiums, and a lawsuit from an angry customer. _____ eventually drove the company into bankruptcy.

3. Rubella, mumps, and polio affect many children in poor countries. Sadly, _____ are preventable, but only if enough money is available for vaccines.

4. The business world was stunned by the company's relocation overseas. It was clear that _____ had been undertaken only as a last resort.

5. Just last month Rudy and Zelda swore they would never date again. And now they've announced they're going to get married. Who could imagine _____!

6. In Coatesville the team's fans overturned cars in the streets. In Glendale they ran onto the field and tore down the goal post. _____ resulted in the team's suspension from the annual tournament.

7. A number of birds that were brought to the United States for their beauty later turned into pests. _____ are the starling and the mute swan.

8. **Patient:** Ever since this project came up, I can't sleep at night, I've lost my appetite, and I'm always grouchy.

   Doctor: _____ are common to stressful situations.

9. The committee searched for a candidate with good credentials and a solid work history. However, _____ could not be found.

10. Abdul works late every night and rarely takes a day off. _____ to his work has earned him a promotion and bonuses, but has also caused some problems with his marriage.

11. You have to get along with people who are not like you. _____ are found everywhere.

12. The candidate loved to meet with people and talk for hours. She would often stay at rallies to discuss issues long after the news reporters went home. She answered her own phone, and spent at least an hour a day reading and responding to letters from worried voters. _____ built her reputation as someone voters could trust.

EXERCISE 10 (Focus 8)

Correct the errors or inappropriate reference forms in each of the following sentences. More than one answer may be possible.

EXAMPLE: Before you leave the building, turn off the lights and lower the thermostat. Such needs to be done before you turn on the burglar alarm.

Correction: *These* need to be done before you turn on the burglar alarm.

1. The speaker last night believed that violent scenes in movies and on TV had a damaging effect on children. He said that violent scenes in movies and on TV dulled children's sense of right and wrong.

2. Dino is the kind of person who is never satisfied with anything, so don't worry about what he said about your paper. This person will always have something unkind to say about anything you do.

3. Did you see the story in the newspaper this morning about the immigrants whose boat sank just as they got near the shore? This story says that most of them swam ashore, but not all of them made it.

4. I had hoped to do my paper on deforestation and its effects on global warming, but someone else had already chosen it.

5. The basketball team acquired veteran forward Vitas Grazinskas. The coach hopes that such a player will help the team a lot.

6. Much classical music has its origins in folk music. One such example of this music is Dvorak's *Slavonic Dances*.

7. **Norma:** I think the drinking age should be lowered to 15.

   Kathy: I disagree with this.

8. **Bob:** What are you going to see tonight?

   Ruben: *Ghost*.

   Bob: But this movie came out years ago—why not see something new?

9. **George:** I read that an advice columnist found that 98 percent of her male readers felt that women had too many rights now. And then on the way to work this morning, I heard a radio talk show host say that 87 percent of his listeners had the same opinion.

   Marian: Come on, George. I heard the exact opposite at a rally I went to last week. It all depends on who you're asking. To be valid, opinion polls have to be random; otherwise these statistics are worthless.

10. One evening last week there were three robberies and one assault on Main Street. It is giving our town a bad reputation.

Choose the one word or phrase that best completes each sentence.

1. Cigarette smoke can damage _____.
   - (A) a lungs
   - (B) lungs
   - (C) lung
   - (D) the lungs

2. Local weather conditions and predictions _____ twenty minutes after the hour, every hour of the day.
   - (A) are reported
   - (B) report
   - (C) are said to report
   - (D) are said to have reported

3. Modern technology has affected our language. _____ can be seen in words like *hookup*, *interface*, and *fax*.
   - (A) That influence
   - (B) The influence
   - (C) Influence
   - (D) This influence

4. Some people feel that the world is designed for their pleasure and ease. _____ can only be considered infantile and ultimately destructive.
   - (A) Such an attitude
   - (B) This people
   - (C) Such as this
   - (D) It

5. _____ are responsible for a large amount of the pollution of urban areas.
   - (A) The automobiles
   - (B) An automobile
   - (C) Automobiles
   - (D) Automobile

6. In ancient Greece, _____ to have been the result of the Titan Atlas's adjusting the earth, which he kept propped up on his mighty shoulders.
   - (A) earthquakes were believed
   - (B) it was believed that earthquakes
   - (C) that earthquakes were believed
   - (D) they were believed the earthquakes

7. The secretary of state _____ to be recovering quickly following a minor operation for the removal of a polyp.
   - (A) said the report
   - (B) the report is said
   - (C) reports
   - (D) is reported

8. A: It's a waste of money to attend state college.
   B: _____ true!
   - (A) This isn't
   - (B) They aren't
   - (C) That isn't
   - (D) These aren't

9. _____ well known for their excellent breakfasts.

    (A) British are

    (B) The British are

    (C) A British is

    (D) British is

10. Luisa's engagement ring _____ by the waiter on the top of the restaurant sink.

    (A) is found

    (B) was discovered

    (C) were found

    (D) are found

11. Hayat has _____ and won't be in school today.

    (A) flu

    (B) cold

    (C) the flu

    (D) the cold

12. Knowledge, a desire to achieve, and an eagerness to work with others are important qualities in a worker. In fact, _____ are more important to the hiring committee than where a person went to school or what grades he or she made.

    (A) qualities

    (B) the qualities

    (C) such qualities

    (D) this

Identify the *one* underlined word or phrase that must be changed for the sentence to be grammatically correct.

13. <u>The tuberculosis</u>, which is <u>a disease</u> primarily of <u>the lungs</u>, appears <u>to be spreading</u> once
       A   **B**   **C**   **D**

again.

14. Dear Mr. President: I have heard or read of many cases of people having operations and

receiving bills for one hundred thousand dollars or more. <u>This situation</u> is terrible. <u>This</u>
                                                                         A

<u>situation</u> is so pernicious that the people in question are often forced to sell their
B

homes. I know you are aware of <u>this</u>. I only pray you can do something about <u>it</u>.
                              C   **D**

15. When I first heard that skunks and raccoons searching for grubs could completely destroy

a lawn, I couldn't believe <u>them</u>. Now that <u>the same thing</u> has happened to my lawn, I
                                  A   **B**

know not to raise <u>such doubt</u> about <u>what</u> at first I don't understand.
                 C   **D**

16. Eighteenth-century <u>wigmakers</u> were also barbers and doctors, which meant that in
                A

addition to making <u>the wigs</u>, they often <u>cut hair</u>, shaved beards, let blood, and <u>pulled teeth</u>.
                     B   **C**   **D**

17. <u>That</u> only Saturn had rings <u>it was presumed</u> <u>to be correct</u> until the transmissions of the
     A   **B**   **C**

Voyager space probes <u>expanded our understanding</u> with startling new data from the outer
                        D

planets.

18. <u>The</u> eastern bobcat, <u>is sometimes known</u> as the bay-lynx, <u>averages</u> fifteen to twenty
     A   **B**   **C**

pounds, although every year a few males in the thirty to thirty-five pound class are taken

<u>by hunters or trappers</u>.
     D

19. <u>Provided that</u> work on the new wing <u>is completed</u> according to plan, we <u>estimate</u> that
     A   **B**   **C**

manufacturing output <u>would have doubled</u> by the end of the next fiscal year.
                        D

20. Some conservationists and tropical biologists are becoming concerned about <u>the survival</u>
                                                                              A

of <u>the strangler fig</u> because its life cycle is fragile and its fruit is <u>a dietary staple</u> of
     B   **C**

<u>the tropical mammals and birds</u>.
     D

21. In a typical system <u>used</u> in advanced surgery and component therapies these days, a
                        A

centrifuge drive, which <u>separates</u> blood into its four components, <u>is connected</u> to various
                        B   **C**

pumps to deliver blood into and out of the system <u>by qualified technicians</u>.
                                                   D

22. <u>The Barbary ape</u> is <u>a small tailless macaque</u> of Algeria, Morocco, and Gibraltar. Legend has
     A   **B**

it that <u>the British</u> will lose the Rock of Gibraltar should its small colony of <u>the Barbary apes</u>
         C   **D**

depart.

23. <u>It's rumor</u> that no less than thirty students <u>are to be</u> <u>dismissed</u> because of <u>cheating</u>.
     A   **B**   **C**   **D**

24. <u>These elephants</u> are <u>the largest land mammals</u>. <u>African elephants</u> are the larger of
     A   **B**   **C**

<u>the two main elephant species</u>.
     D

25. Participating in <u>normally enjoyable sports</u> can have <u>dire consequences</u> when people fail
                     A   **B**

to exercise caution or lose control. <u>Such two sports</u> are skiing and sailing. Sheer
                                     C

negligence is responsible for many accidents in <u>these</u> sports.
                                                 D

UNIT

7 Relative Clauses Modifying Subjects

(Focus 1)

Complete the relative clauses of the sentences below using the information given about the following three small countries.

LIECHTENSTEIN

Population: 30,000

Government: Monarchy

Prime Minister: Hans Brunhart

Location: between Austria and Switzerland

Income: $22,300 per person

Capital: Vaduz—population 4,874

Brief history: The country was founded in 1719. It abolished the army in 1868, yet remained undamaged by any of Europe's wars since that time. The country is closely related to Switzerland, whose currency it uses. There is no unemployment, and taxes are low. Liechtenstein today has the distinction of being the world's largest exporter of false teeth.

NAURU

Population: 9,500

Government: Parliamentary

President: Bernard Dowiyogo

Location: Pacific Ocean, 2,500 miles southwest of Hawaii

Income: $10,000 per person

Capital: Yaren—population 5,590

Brief history: The island was annexed to the German Empire in 1886. After World War I, the island was administered by Australia. During World War II, Japan occupied the island. In 1947, Nauru was put under the trust of the United Nations, and again administered by Australia. Finally, on January 31, 1968, Nauru became an independent state. There are no taxes on the island, and the literacy rate is 99 percent.

SAN MARINO

Population: 20,000

Government: Republic

Co-regents: elected every six months

Location: Northern Italy

Income: $17,000 per person

Capital: San Marino—population 2,339

Brief history: According to tradition, San Marino has been in existence for over 16 centuries, making it the oldest state in Europe and the oldest republic in the world. Although it has a tradition of peaceful government and friendly relations, the country has been politically active, losing two soldiers in World War I, being occupied by the Nazis (and bombed by the allies) during World War II, and today maintaining a standing army of 80 soldiers. Although the economy is diverse, its largest source of income is the sale of postage stamps to collectors.

EXAMPLE: The country ___that___ has the highest standard of living is
Liechtenstein._____.

1. The country _____ is located in the Pacific Ocean is _____.

2. The country _____ is actually the oldest in Europe is _____.

3. The only country _____ is governed by a president is _____. The
   other countries are governed by a prime minister and co-regents.

4. The country _____ was administered by Australia for over 50 years is
   _____.

5. The country _____ uses the Swiss franc is _____.

6. The country _____ stamp collectors love to go to is _____.

7. The country _____ lost two soldiers in World War II is _____.

8. The country _____ became an independent state in 1968 is
   _____.

9. The country _____ the Nazis occupied _____ in World War II is
   _____.

EXERCISE 2   (Focus 1)

Complete the following by combining the sentence pairs using a relative clause.

EXAMPLE: The American president was assassinated in 1963. He was John F. Kennedy.

The American president __who was assassinated in 1963_____

__was John F. Kennedy._____

1. I gave money to a charitable organization. It turned out to be a fraud.
   The charitable organization _____.

2. I bought a synthesizer last week. It is now on sale.
   The synthesizer _____.

3. The company is probably going to be sold. Its employees are on strike.
   The company _____.

4. The cat has been hanging around our house. I rescued it from a tree.
   The cat _____.

5. People may have poor diets. They tend to get sick often.
   People _____.

6. You saw the young student in the hall with the dean. He's actually working on a doctorate in mathematics.

The young student _____.

7. The painter just got another grant. His works were featured in last week's *Time* magazine.

The painter _____.

8. The woman used to work with your mother. You gave your seat to her.

The woman _____.

9. A company should take an honest look at itself. Its employees are always complaining.

A company _____.

EXERCISE 3   (*Focus 2*)

Make all the simple descriptions of the pictures more specific by adding a relative clause to each.

EXAMPLE: The man is a diplomat.

The man who is on the phone at the desk

is a diplomat.

1. The man is a diplomat.

_____

2. The students are all honor students.

_____

3. The man tries to work out everyday.

_____

4. The woman is a park police officer.

_____

Following are nine items that many people consider necessary for a long and happy life. For each item, add a relative clause that specifies the qualities of these items.

EXAMPLE: a job

A job that pays a reasonable salary and is personally

rewarding is necessary for a long and happy life.

1. a spouse

_____

_____

2. housing

_____

_____

3. children

_____

_____

4. friends

_____

_____

5. leisure time

_____

_____

6. a hobby

_____

_____

7. an education

_____

_____

8. a boss

_____

_____

9. a neighborhood

_____

_____

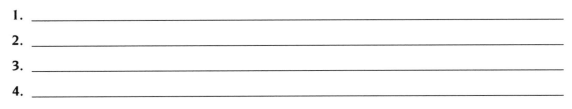

EXERCISE 5 (Focus 3)

Look at the sentences you wrote in Exercise 3. Delete all unnecessary words to reduce the relative clause.

1. _____

2. _____

3. _____

4. _____

EXERCISE 6 (Focus 3)

Where possible, reduce the relative clauses in the following sentences and make any other necessary changes.

1. The manager whom we met was very polite.

   _____

   _____

2. The computer which is at the end of the row is out of order.

   _____

   _____

3. The crowd cheered the runner who was trying to regain the lead.

   _____

   _____

4. Students who are dedicated can be found in the library on Saturday nights.

   _____

   _____

5. Customers who do not have their receipts cannot return their merchandise.

   _____

   _____

6. The paintings which we saw at the museum were impressive.

   _____

   _____

7. The president who was elected in November saw his popularity decline in March.

   _____

   _____

8. The parking place which is near the entrance is reserved for the employee of the month.

_____

_____

9. Workers who were angry confronted the union leader about the new contract.

_____

_____

10. Programmers who have experience with UNIX systems will be given first consideration.

_____

_____

EXERCISE 7 (Focus 3)

Rewrite these sentences, reducing the relative clauses, to uncover the common sayings.

EXAMPLE: The bird who is early catches the worm.

The early bird catches the worm. _____

1. You can't teach a dog that is old new tricks.

_____

2. A bird that is in the hand is worth two in the bush.

_____

3. A workman who is bad blames his tools.

_____

4. People who are in glass houses shouldn't throw stones.

_____

5. A stone that is rolling gathers no moss.

_____

6. A pot that is watched never boils.

_____

UNIT 8 Relative Clauses Modifying Objects

EXERCISE 1 (*Focus 1*)

Complete the crossword puzzle.

ACROSS

1. That journalist is a person _____ ideas I have a hard time understanding.
2. She asked us _____ whom we were going to dine.
3. I have no idea _____ you're talking about. Is it Hannah?
4. Kant is a philosopher _____ whom I know very little.
6. That is a place which I will never go _____.

DOWN

1. The jury was finally shown the evidence, _____ the lawyer had alluded to.
3. Thomas Jefferson was a practical man _____ had a great deal of ingenuity.
4. Over in the corner there is a strange person _____ whom the children are staring.
5. Have you seen the movie _____ is playing at the Paramount?

Combine the pairs of sentences below using relative pronouns.

EXAMPLE:　The catapult was an ancient military weapon. It was used for hurling missiles.

The catapult was an ancient military weapon which was used for hurling missiles.

1. I wanted to meet the famous singer. My brother had once interviewed him.

_____

_____

_____

2. We phoned our neighbors. We left our dog with them.

_____

_____

_____

3. We were awed by the mountain. From its summit flowed four great glaciers.

_____

_____

_____

4. I looked in vain for my keys. I thought I had put them in my briefcase.

_____

_____

_____

5. Gloria photographed the dolphin. She had thrown some fish to it.

_____

_____

_____

Write definitions for the items in column A by combining information from both columns B and C with relative pronouns. The first one is done below as an example.

A	B	C
1. surgeon	**A.** process	**a.** It is used to detect and record seismic waves caused by earthquakes
2. computer	**B.** award	
3. irrigation	**C.** science	**b.** their necks can be spread to form a hood when alarmed
4. seismograph	**D.** treeless plains in the Arctic Circle	**c.** it is prepared from vegetable or animal fats
5. Nobel Prize	**E.** device	
6. cobras	**F.** instrument	**d.** he or she performs operations
7. entomology	**G.** spread	**e.** its soil is a thin coating over permafrost
8. tundra	**H.** horse race	
9. margarine	**I.** doctor	**f.** it is given to individuals from all over the world who have made outstanding contributions in their fields
10. Kentucky Derby	**J.** poisonous snakes	
		g. it is devoted to the study of insects
		h. it performs calculations
		i. in this race three-year-old horses run over a one-and-a-quarter mile course at Churchill Downs in Louisville, Kentucky
		j. water is artificially conducted to soil to promote growth by this process

1. *A surgeon is a doctor who performs operations.*

2. _____

3. _____

4. _____

5. _____

6. _____

7. _____

8. _____

9. _____

10. _____

    The following pictures and descriptions relate to fantastic creatures and monsters of ancient Greek mythology. Use each picture to provide the first relative clause and join it with the information provided to make one sentence with multiple relative clauses.

EXAMPLE:

Every year fourteen victims were sacrificed to the Minotaur. He lived in a labyrinth under the palace of King Minos of Crete.

Every year fourteen victims were
sacrificed to the Minotaur, who was
half-man and half-bull and lived under
the palace of King Minos of Crete.

1. People were frightened of griffins. These monsters destroyed anyone who strayed into their territory.

2. The most frightening of the three Gorgon sisters was Medusa. Medusa's glance could turn a man to stone.

3. The gates to the underworld were guarded by Cerberus. The dog threatened anyone who came too close.

4. As one of their tortures, the gods used the Harpies. The Harpies' claws tore at their unfortunate victims.

5. The monster that lay in wait for travelers on the road to Thebes was the Sphinx. The Sphinx dared those she stopped to solve a riddle or die.

6. Ulysses killed the Cyclops. The Cyclops lived in a cave above the shore and ate sheep and men.

7. Ulysses was fortunate to escape from Circe. It was her pleasure to turn men into swine.

8. Ships were often wrecked because of the Sirens. Their irresistible song lured sailors to their doom.

9. Perseus was the hero who killed the Chimera. It had both a lion's and a goat's head and the body of a dragon with a snake for a tail.

10. For the ancient Greeks the only monsters who were essentially good were the Centaurs. The Centaurs became rude and uncontrollable only when they became intoxicated with wine.

1. _____

_____

2. _____

_____

3. _____

_____

4. _____

_____

5. _____

_____

6. _____

_____

7. _____

_____

8. _____

_____

9. _____

_____

10. _____

Rewrite the following sentences, deleting relative pronouns where possible.

EXAMPLE: The professor graded all the papers which we submitted last week.

The professor graded all the papers we submitted last week.

1. I am often disappointed in movies which are made from books I have enjoyed.

   _____

   _____

2. We rented the same house which our friends had lived in last year.

   _____

   _____

3. Look at the deer that are hiding in the shadows!

   _____

   _____

4. The students were frustrated by the computer program which mysteriously deleted much of their data.

   _____

   _____

5. I felt overwhelmed by the papers which were scattered all over my room.

   _____

   _____

6. The trekkers walked down a narrow trail that had a terrifying drop.

   _____

   _____

7. So far we haven't found a candidate who is competent enough to get the job.

   _____

   _____

8. Doris forgot to thank the woman whom she had received a gift from.

   _____

   _____

9. Where can I buy a cup of coffee that is not overpriced?

   _____

   _____

10. I went to the restaurant that you recommended.

_____

_____

EXERCISE 6 (Focus 4)

Look again at the answers you wrote for Exercise 3. Rewrite the sentences in which relative pronouns can be deleted. If no deletion is possible, write NO on the line provided.

1. _____

2. _____

3. _____

4. _____

5. _____

6. _____

7. _____

8. _____

9. _____

10. _____

EXERCISE 7 (Focus 5)

Rewrite the last sentence in each short dialog, changing it, if possible, to more formal English. Indicate where no change is possible.

EXAMPLE: **Lawyer:** Do you have the necessary papers?

Client: Here are the deeds that you referred to.

Here are the deeds to which you referred.

1. Ali: Consider the achievements of the Arabs in mathematics, architecture, and literature.

Nancy: The Arabs have a culture that they are justifiably proud of.

_____

2. Art: Do you happen to know where the MaxTech company is?

Betty: It's a tiny office that they work out of.

_____

3. **Mrs. Phillips:** All the applicants for the special grant seem rather weak this year.

   Mr. Cabot: I absolutely agree. I don't think there are any that we can award it to.

---

4. **Student:** Please, sir, could you repeat what you just said?

   Professor Said: This is a seminar that we shall discuss nineteenth-century colonialism in.

---

5. **Craig:** Do you actually think we shall have to go back to where we started from?

   Eleanor: I'm afraid this is an obstacle that we cannot get around.

---

6. **Carol:** Amanda seems peevish when she doesn't get her way.

   Brenda: That's because she was a girl who nothing was ever denied to.

---

7. **Deepak:** Modern biology could not exist without the contributions of Charles Darwin.

   Chandra: Darwin was a scientist that we all owe a debt to.

---

8. **Klaus:** What have you discovered regarding the sixth Baron of Munchausen?

   Frederic: Apparently he was a recluse who nothing is known about.

---

9. **Corinne:** Do you know about *Antaeus*, *Parabola*, and the *Bloomsbury Review*?

   Sylvia: Of course, they are all magazines that I subscribe to.

---

10. **Husband:** Your cousins from Chicago said they'd like to come and stay with us for a few days.

    Wife: That's not going to be possible. They are a family that we just cannot put up.

Rewrite the following sentences to make them less formal.

EXAMPLE: Here is another letter from the young man whom we rejected.

Here is another letter from the young man we rejected.

1. Here is a challenge to which I hope you will rise.

_____

2. Sam went to hear the music group whom your parents dislike.

_____

3. There are a number of scams about which we have been warned.

_____

4. Paul tried to avoid the man to whom he owed some money.

_____

5. Tony Blair is a politician about whom everyone is talking.

_____

6. I found the letter which she tried to hide.

_____

7. The principal sent a message to the students whom the teachers failed.

_____

8. Helen of Troy was a beautiful woman for whom many Greek warriors sacrificed their lives.

_____

9. Racial superiority is an idea to which no intelligent person can subscribe.

_____

10. I remember the passage about which you are speaking.

_____

11. It was a very small, old man at which the children were staring.

_____

UNIT 9 Nonrestrictive Relative Clauses

Complete the sentences below using a restrictive relative clause in (a) and a nonrestrictive relative clause in (b).

EXAMPLE: **(a)** The violin _that was used by Beethoven himself_ sold for $1,000,000.

(b) The violin, _which is an instrument I love_, takes years to learn to play well.

1. **(a)** The cellular phone _____ hasn't been as good as I had hoped.

   (b) Cellular phones, _____, are banned in certain restaurants.

2. **(a)** If you want more information you'll have to consult the data base _____.

   (b) If you want more information you'll have to consult a data base, _____.

3. **(a)** The McDonald's _____ is a favorite place for students to meet.

   (b) McDonald's, _____, is the largest restaurant chain in the world.

4. **(a)** The dog _____ once saved a child's life.

   (b) The dog, _____, has often proved useful to people.

5. **(a)** Clouds _____ are called fog.

   (b) My younger sister loves to lie on the grass and look at clouds, _____.

6. **(a)** I got an A on the paper _____.

   (b) The history paper I turned in, _____, got an A.

7. **(a)** The encyclopedia _____ has just been shipped.

   (b) The encyclopedia, _____, has evolved over the centuries.

8. (a) Personal computers _____ are needed to run many new programs.

(b) Personal computers, _____, are found almost everywhere in the world today.

9. (a) The fax machine _____ frequently has a long line of people waiting to use it.

(b) The fax machine, _____, is used by children in Japan to exchange messages and compare homework assignments.

10. (a) The horse _____ was trained by my uncle.

(b) The horse, _____, was first domesticated over 2,500 years ago.

EXERCISE 2 (*Focus 2*)

You are a new student at a college, living away from home, writing a letter to your good friend Chris. You are including information about the following: the school, the students, your advanced English course, your English teacher, the town, and your living situation. Below are a group of nonrestrictive relative clauses. Find the best places to put them in the letter that follows. You will also have to add information of your own and punctuate correctly.

(a) with whom I had a nice talk today at lunch

(b) which is a pleasant community

(c) which has four rooms in addition to a living room, kitchen, and bathroom

(d) which I check every day

(e) which has an enrollment of five thousand

(f) all of whom are students

(g) who come from all over the world

(h) whose courses, I understand, are very popular

(i) all of which makes for some stimulating discussion

(j) which is a place I've always wanted to visit

(k) which so far has been challenging and quite interesting

Dear Chris,

I'm sorry I haven't written in a while but life has been very busy these last weeks as I try to settle into college and a new routine. Let me tell you a little about the school, the advanced English course I'm taking, the town and the place where I'm living.

The school _____.

The students, _____, are

_____ with many ideas,

_____. I'm taking an advanced English course

_____. My English teacher

_____ is from San Francisco

_____ and has taught in

_____. I feel fortunate to have this teacher

_____.

   The school is located _____. I managed to find a place

to live _____.

I share _____.

   That's all for now. I'll write more when I get the chance. Send

_____. I hope that everything is well with you and your

family.

   Your friend,

EXERCISE 3   (Focus 3)

   Below are tools, instruments, and accessories from various fields. Describe the object and identify a field it typically is used in.

EXAMPLE: *The microscope, which is an optical instrument with a lens or a combination of lenses that magnify small objects, is used in scientific and medical research.*

1. stethoscope

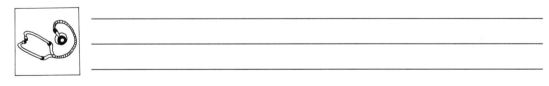

2. hammer

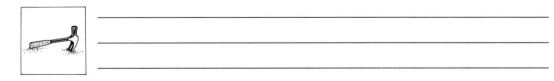

3. spatula

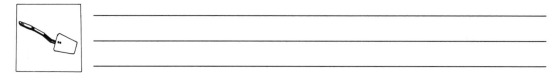

_____

_____

_____

_____

4. hoe

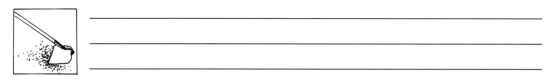

_____

_____

_____

_____

5. handcuffs

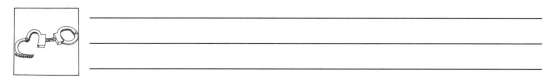

_____

_____

_____

_____

6. compass

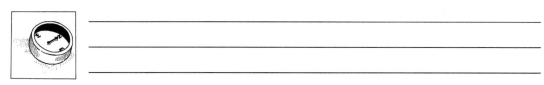

_____

_____

_____

_____

7. tripod

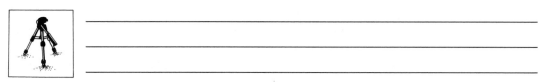

_____

_____

_____

_____

8. periodic table

_____

_____

_____

_____

9. wrench

_____

_____

_____

_____

10. scalpel

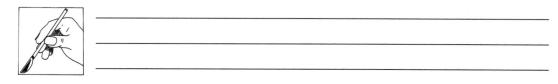

_____

_____

_____

EXERCISE 4   (Focus 4)

Below is an informal story that Lydia is telling about her recent trip. Fill in the blanks with nonrestrictive relative clauses.

EXAMPLE: I made a photocopy of my passport before I left, **which was smart.**

(1) I also put all of my money into traveler's checks, _____.
(2) However, I forgot to make notes of which checks I had spent, _____, because of what happened later. **(3)** I left my purse in the hotel room while I went downstairs for breakfast, _____.
(4) When I got back to the room, I found the door open and my purse missing, _____, so I called the manager. **(5)** She said someone had stolen one of the master keys to the hotel, but she had not changed the locks yet, _____. **(6)** When I asked her why she hadn't done this, she said she had hoped it wouldn't be a problem, _____. **(7)** The thief had stolen not just my purse with all my money and my passport, but also my camera, and the watch that my mother had given to me for my eighteenth birthday, _____. **(8)** When I asked the manager if she would help me replace any of the stolen items, she said it wasn't her fault, _____ so much that I left without paying.

(9) Outside the hotel, I called to report my stolen traveler's checks, and the agent was very helpful, _____. **(10)** However, because I couldn't tell her which checks had been stolen and which had been spent, I could only cancel the checks I knew I hadn't spent, _____. **(11)** My passport replacement wasn't very difficult; I just went to the embassy with my photocopy, and they gave me a new passport that afternoon, _____.

Lydia is still talking about her trip. Fill in the relevant information using quantifiers in each nonrestrictive noun clause given.

EXAMPLE: I visited several countries and really enjoyed meeting the local people, **_most of whom_** were very friendly.

(1) In Italy, I visited a number of art galleries, _____ contained Boticelli's *Birth of Venus*. **(2)** After I had so many problems staying in hotels, _____ I enjoyed, I decided to stay in hostels, _____ were cheaper than even the lowest priced hotels. **(3)** The hostels in France were especially nice, _____ was a converted seventeenth-century monastery. **(4)** The other people in the hostels, _____ were from Europe, Japan, or Australia, were fun to be with, and had a lot of good ideas about places I should see next. **(5)** I especially liked the Australians, _____ I traveled to England with. **(6)** In London we visited the British Museum and the Victoria and Albert Museum, _____ we loved. **(7)** We also traveled north to the Lake District, where we hiked through several small towns, _____ was the home of the poet Wordsworth. **(8)** The Australians had relatives all over the country, _____ had an apartment in Edinburgh, so we went north to stay with her for a night. **(9)** She introduced us to some of her friends, _____ took us to a place that had all-night dancing.

Complete the crossword puzzle by finding the words that correctly fill in the blanks.

ACROSS

2. I have many good friends, _____ of whom I love dearly.
3. Simon dated three young women in the last three months, two of _____ he found very charming.
6. The student handed in two essays, _____ of which need to be revised. (Each one had many errors.)
7. There were three small guest houses in the village, none _____ which accepted credit cards.
8. She had to choose between two candidates, _____ of which she particularly liked. (She didn't like one or the other.)

DOWN

1. Paula read three mystery novels recently, _____ of which she enjoyed. (She enjoyed every one of them.)
3. We have nine rooms in our house, three of _____ need new carpets.
4. In my class there's Paul, Peter, Bonny, Kathy, Diane, and Tim, _____ of whom has blue eyes. (They all have brown eyes.)
5. I read several reviews of the film, _____ of which were good. (The critics were divided in their opinion of the film.)

TOEFL®

Test Preparation Exercises
Units 7–9

Choose the one word or phrase that best completes each sentence.

1. The workmen cut down the tree _____ trunk was infested with insects.
   - (A) whose
   - (B) which
   - (C) that
   - (D) of which

2. The student _____ won the contest received a $1,000 scholarship.
   - (A) that his essay
   - (B) who his essay
   - (C) which essay
   - (D) whose essay

3. The archeologists uncovered _____ an ancient tribe had buried.
   - (A) the chests
   - (B) whose chests
   - (C) of which chests
   - (D) the chests of which

4. I brought home a wounded pigeon I found in the street, _____ was not a good idea.
   - (A) that
   - (B) who
   - (C) which
   - (D) where

5. The joke _____ made Chris upset.
   - (A) that I thought was so funny
   - (B) which I thought it was so funny
   - (C) I thought that was so funny
   - (D) I thought it was so funny

6. A doctor _____ only on back pain is called a chiropractor.
   - (A) whom works
   - (B) which works
   - (C) works
   - (D) who works

7. I enjoyed very little of the book _____ so many glowing reviews had been written.
   - (A) which
   - (B) whose
   - (C) about which
   - (D) at that

8. Singapore, _____ is a city-state just south of Malaysia, has a total ban on chewing gum in public.
   - (A) that
   - (B) who
   - (C) which
   - (D) where

9. The corporations _____ were interested in our project.
   - (A) which we spoke
   - (B) we spoke
   - (C) to which we spoke
   - (D) which to we spoke

10. Pangaea is the name given to the primeval supercontinent _____, due to tectonic activity of the plates, split up to form Laurasia in the northern hemisphere and Gondwanaland in the southern hemisphere.

    (A) from which   (C) where

    (B) of whose   (D) which

Identify the *one* underlined word or phrase that must be changed for the sentence to be grammatically correct.

11. The Bolshoi <u>which</u> classical ballet and opera productions <u>have</u> a worldwide reputation
           A   **B**

    <u>possesses</u> a stage <u>that</u> is one of the largest in the world.
      C   **D**

12. If you're intending to take courses <u>that</u> will lead to a science degree, <u>you probably</u>
                              A   **B**

    <u>shouldn't</u> neglect to take a few liberal arts courses, <u>all which</u> will provide you with an
                                           C

    important cultural background <u>as well as</u> practice at expressing yourself clearly.
                             D

13. Were you aware that <u>the man with you</u> spoke yesterday <u>at the reception</u> was a Nobel prize
                         A   **B**

    winner <u>whose research</u> in medicine <u>has led to</u> a whole new generation of cancer-
           C   **D**

    inhibiting drugs?

14. <u>Taking advantage of the fact that</u> masses of air often flow upward, <u>creating a force</u> called
              A   **B**

    lift, large birds can hitch a ride on a current of air and glide for hours <u>without flapping</u>
                                                       C

    their wings. Lift, <u>that acts as</u> a kind of escalator to the clouds, comes in several different
                   D

    forms.

15. When she was later asked <u>about it</u>, the former hostage said <u>that</u> the <u>thing which for</u> she
                          A   **B**   **C**

    would <u>always be grateful was</u> her freedom.
             D

16. After Joan's first computer class she <u>remained at her desk and gazed</u> with tired eyes at
                                A

    the long list of keyboard commands, <u>of whose functions</u> she could no longer remember,
                                B

    and wondered <u>if she would ever</u> get the hang of <u>such a</u> complex machine.
                 C   **D**

17. Galaxies <u>whose low surface brightness due to</u> fewer stars, were, in the past, <u>considered</u>
                     A   **B**

dwarfs. Recently astronomers <u>have found that</u> the actual mass of <u>many of them</u> is
                                C   **D**

considerably larger than suspected.

18. Esperanto, <u>which</u> an artificial language <u>created by</u> Dr. L. L. Zamenhof, <u>who was</u> from
               A   **B**   **C**

Poland, <u>was meant to enable</u> people of different linguistic backgrounds to communicate
          D

more easily.

19. The researchers found <u>that it was</u> nicotine, <u>of which</u> is a colorless oily liquid <u>that</u> occurs
                               A   **B**   **C**

in tobacco, <u>that was</u> responsible for raising blood pressure and impairing digestion.
             D

20. Why was it <u>that</u> they couldn't find anyone <u>who was</u> both capable and inspiring and <u>who</u>
                A   **B**   **C**

could still get the job done <u>which in a way</u> would not destroy his personal life?
                                     D

UNIT 10 Relative Adverb Clauses

EXERCISE 1 (Focus 1)

Complete the crossword puzzle.

ACROSS

1. When you are in a foreign land, you may have culture shock if you can't accept the _____ people do things there.
2. There are not many schools in _____ you can get an advanced degree in only a year.
5. The _____ why the exam was canceled was because the power was out.
6. The intermission is a time _____ which we can get refreshments.

DOWN

1. The house _____ we are living is a rambling Victorian structure.
2. 1967 was the year _____ Jerry was born.
3. I don't know _____ my parents felt, but I was sad the day we moved.
4. The town _____ which we began our walk was built in the Middle Ages.

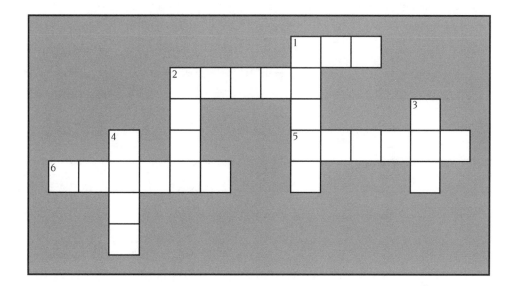

Substitute relative adverbials for prepositions + *which* whenever possible and make other necessary changes.

EXAMPLE: The Christmas season, during which some retailers do more than half of their annual business, is the busiest holiday in the United States.

The Christmas season, when some retailers do more than half of

their annual business, is the busiest holiday in the United States.

1. The day on which Christmas is celebrated for Protestants and Roman Catholics was set by the Roman Church in 336 A.D.

2. One of the reasons for which December 25 was chosen was a preexisting festival in the ancient Zoroastrian religion.

3. Early Christian leaders were worried about the way in which Zoroastrians practiced their religion because of its resemblance to Christian rites.

4. They hoped that the way in which they overlapped the holidays would enable Zoroastrians to easily convert to Christianity.

5. Christmas grew into a commonly accepted festival in the Middle Ages, during which it became so popular that certain Christians objected to some of its rituals.

6. Early Protestants in particular disliked the manner in which Christmas was celebrated, leading to a ban on Christmas in England for part of the seventeenth century.

_____

_____

_____

7. Santa Claus is the name which eighteenth-century New Yorkers gave to Saint Nicholas, a fourth-century bishop from Asia Minor (now Turkey).

_____

_____

_____

8. The feast of Saint Nicholas, the patron saint of children, was celebrated on a holiday apart from Christmas, on December 6, at which time someone dressed as the bishop and distributed presents to small children.

_____

_____

_____

9. There were many reasons for which the two holidays, Saint Nicholas's feast day and Christmas, merged.

_____

_____

_____

10. In general, both holidays have themes of gratitude and generosity, especially toward children, which might account for the way in which December 25 now is marked by an infant (Christ) and a large man in a red suit who gives presents to children (Santa Claus).

_____

_____

_____

PART A

Match each of the time periods in the first column with an event in the second column. Then write complete sentences, using relative adverbials + an appropriate head noun.

EXAMPLE: July 4 / Americans celebrate their independence

July 4 is the day when Americans celebrate their independence.

1. Ramadan	**a.** World War II ended
2. Asian lunar New Year	**b.** many workers stop for lunch
3. The nineteenth century	**c.** the first Japanese constitution was written
4. 1969	**d.** Muslims refrain from eating in the daytime
5. From noon to one o'clock	**e.** most Asians cook delicious meals and give gifts of money
6. 1945	**f.** Queen Victoria ruled Great Britain
7. Winter	**g.** Neil Armstrong became the first person to walk on` the moon
8. The Meiji Restoration	**h.** people go skiing

1. _____
2. _____
3. _____
4. _____
5. _____
6. _____
7. _____
8. _____

PART B

Match each place in the first column with an event in the second column. Then write complete sentences, using relative adverbials + an appropriate head noun. Try to use nouns other than *place* if possible.

EXAMPLE: Istanbul / Europe and Asia meet

Istanbul is the city where Europe and Asia meet.

1. downstairs   **a.** the 1978 and 1986 World Cup champions are from here

2. Mecca   **b.** people are buried here

3. north   **c.** a government meets in this building

4. Saudi Arabia   **e.** a house is coolest here

5. the capitol   **f.** a compass needle points here

6. a cemetery   **g.** every Muslim must make a pilgrimage

7. Argentina   **h.** about one-third of all the world's oil is located here

1. _____
2. _____
3. _____
4. _____
5. _____
6. _____
7. _____

PART C

Match each reason in the first column with a statement in the second column. Then write complete sentences.

EXAMPLE: its strength and light weight / titanium is used in aircraft because of this

Its strength and light weight are reasons why titanium is used in aircraft.

1. a chance for a better life   **a.** the ozone layer is healing because of this

2. their better gas mileage   **b.** sharks have no natural predators because of this

3. its irregular spelling   **c.** people immigrate for this

4. higher worker productivity   **d.** people buy compact cars for this

5. their size and aggressive behavior   **e.** people like Charlie Chaplin for this

6. decreased use of fluorocarbons   **f.** written English can be difficult because of this

7. his sense of humor   **g.** businesses use machines for this

1. _____
2. _____
3. _____

4. _____

5. _____

6. _____

7. _____

PART D

Match the processes or methods in the first column with a statement in the second column. Then write complete sentences, using either the head noun *way* or the adverb *how*.

EXAMPLE: studying hard / most top students make top grades

Studying hard is how most top students make top grades.

OR

Studying hard is the way most top students make top grades.

1. weight training

2. letting cilantro go to seed

3. giving a press conference

4. an overtime period of five minutes

5. inattention to details

6. good customer service

7. cutting back on the use of fossil fuels

a. projects fail because of this

b. clients are kept by giving this

c. athletes build strength this way

d. you get coriander in this manner

e. politicians disseminate information this way

f. the atmosphere will remain clean if we do this

g. basketball games tied at the end are decided this way

1. _____

2. _____

3. _____

4. _____

5. _____

6. _____

7. _____

Complete the sentences below using a relative adverb without a head noun and any other necessary words.

      EXAMPLE: <u>This is how</u>_____ you put a new roll of film in the camera.

1. _____ I am studying English.

2. I have always wondered about _____.

3. _____ my parents were married.

4. I have never understood _____.

5. _____ I usually go to bed.

6. _____ I lived when I was a child.

Match each of the places and times in the first column with the events in the second column. Write complete sentences using relative adverbs without head nouns.

      EXAMPLE: Egypt / the great pyramids are here

        <u>*Egypt is where the great pyramids are located.*</u>

1. 1990	**a.** Asian lunar New Year falls
2. Italy	**b.** the world's tallest mountains are found here
3. 7 to 9 A.M. and 4 to 6 P.M.	**c.** the Berlin Wall fell
4. February 14	**d.** Valentine's Day is celebrated
5. between January 21 and February 19	**e.** Ferrari, Alfa-Romeo, and Lamborghini cars are made here
6. evening	**f.** rush hour occurs in many large cities
7. Nepal	**g.** people eat dinner

1. _____

2. _____

3. _____

4. _____

5. _____

6. _____

7. _____

PART A

Rewrite six of the sentences used in Exercise 3 (two each from Parts A, B, and C) using the form of head noun without relative adverbial. Make any other necessary changes.

EXAMPLE: North is the direction where a compass needle points.

North is the direction a compass needle points to.

1. _____

2. _____

3. _____

4. _____

5. _____

6. _____

PART B

Rewrite four of the sentences used in Exercise 5 using the form of head noun without relative adverbial. Make any other necessary changes.

EXAMPLE: 1990 is when the Berlin Wall fell.

1990 is the year the Berlin Wall fell.

1. _____

2. _____

3. _____

4. _____

Decide whether the form given in (a) or (b) would be more typical or appropriate for each context. Explain your choice by referring to one of the conditions below.

A HEAD NOUN IS USED

   a. To focus on or emphasize time, place, reason, or manner

   b. When the meaning of the head noun is specific

   c. When the context is more formal

   d. When the head noun is the subject of a sentence rather than part of the predicate

A HEAD NOUN IS NOT USED

   e. When the meaning of the head noun's phrase is general

   f. When we can infer the head noun from the context or from general knowledge

   g. When the context is informal

1. This special day is _____ families come together from all over the country.
   (a) a time when   **(b)** when   Condition: _____

2. I'm sorry to have to call you into my office, but I must tell you that _____ is unacceptable.
   (a) the manner in which you have behaved   **(b)** how you behaved   Condition: _____

3. **Bella:** Do you remember when Ingrid is coming?
   Luigi: Let me think...oh yes, she's coming _____ I'll be out of town.
   (a) when   **(b)** during the week in which Condition: _____

4. Do you know _____ the mail comes?
   (a) the time in which   **(b)** when   Condition: _____

5. Did Jane say _____ she wasn't coming?
   (a) why   **(b)** the reason for which   Condition: _____

6. Greta showed me _____ I could buy stylish and inexpensive clothes.
   (a) a second-hand store where   **(b)** where   Condition: _____

7. _____ students could study in groups would be nice.
   (a) A place where   **(b)** Where   Condition: _____

8. The thieves drew a map of _____ they buried the money.
   (a) where   **(b)** the cemetery where   Condition: _____

9. _____ did you want me to make your coffee, dear?
   (a) In what manner   **(b)** How   Condition: _____

10. November is _____ Americans celebrate Thanksgiving.
   (a) when   **(b)** the month when   Condition: _____

Fill in the blanks with relative adverbials or a head noun + a relative adverbial.

EXAMPLE: Bhutan is a remote country in the Himalayas, __*a country which*__ until recent years has remained closed to most tourists.

1. They began their trip in April, _____ the flowers were beginning to bloom and the world was beautiful.

2. We had a great vacation in the Caribbean, _____ the temperature was 20 degrees warmer than it was here.

3. 1968 was a significant year in U.S. history, _____ both Martin Luther King and Robert Kennedy were assassinated, and U.S. troops sustained a major defeat in Vietnam.

4. I'll never forget my childhood, _____ I didn't have to worry about work or bills.

5. While we were in Taipei we visited the Palace Museum, _____ we saw, among other things, a cabbage that was made of jade.

EXERCISE 9 (*Focus 5*)

Complete the sentences beginning with a relative adverbial and then with ideas from your own general knowledge and imagination.

1. The caravan set out to cross the Sahara desert, _____

_____.

2. The fourteenth century was a harsh time, _____

_____.

3. The expedition began its bid to conquer Mount Everest, _____

_____.

4. The next century promises to be a tumultuous one, _____

_____.

5. I felt nervous entering the large empty house, _____

_____.

UNIT 11

Correlative Conjunctions

EXERCISE 1 (Focus 1)

Andy Morgan recently participated in a survey. Some of the questions asked are reproduced below along with the survey-taker's notes. Make at least seven sentences using correlative conjunctions for emphasis.

EXAMPLE: *While on vacation Andy and Emily Morgan like both to meet people and to use other languages.*

Does anyone in your household smoke? No

How many members of your household work? He, wife (Emily)

Do you have any children? Son, daughter. Grown up.

Do you plan to make any major purchases within the coming year? Car

What make? Undecided. Dodge/Toyota

Do you subscribe to any magazines? Newsweek, The Atlantic Monthly, National Geographic, Home

Where are you planning to spend your next vacation? Undecided. Mexico/Brazil

What do you like to do on vacation? Explore / meet people / use other languages / try different foods / snorkel / walk

1. _____

   _____

2. _____

   _____

3. _____

   _____

4. _____

   _____

5. _____

   _____

6. _____

_____

7. _____

_____

EXERCISE 2 (Focus 1)

As the manager of data operations for a small company, you need to hire someone to join your team of hardware and software experts. Evaluate the qualifications of the applicants below. Respond to the questions using correlative conjunctions for emphasis.

Tony Perez	Emma Singh	Laura Park
B.S. in electrical engineering	B.S. in computer information systems	B.S. in electrical engineering
Experience with DOS and UNIX systems	Experience with DOS and UNIX systems	Experience with DOS
3 years' experience as programmer	6 years' experience as programmer	8 years' experience as programmer
Trained in microcomputer repair	Not trained in microcomputer repair	Trained in microcomputer repair
Proficient in PASCAL	Proficient in PASCAL	Proficient in FORTRAN
Advanced knowledge of circuit design	Proficient in C	M.B.A
Can start immediately	Can start by the first of the month	Can start at the end of the year
Applied to this company before	First-time applicant	First-time applicant
Extensive experience in mainframe software and design	Most experience limited to microcomputers	Most experience limited to microcomputers

EXAMPLE: Do any of the applicants have engineering backgrounds?

Yes, both Tony Perez and Laura Park have B.S. degrees in electrical engineering.

1. Does either Tony Perez or Laura Park have an advanced degree in engineering?

_____

_____

2. Can any of the applicants work in UNIX?

_____

_____

3. If I wanted someone who knew how to fix computers as well as use them, who could I hire?

_____

_____

4. Do any of the applicants have more than 5 years' experience in programming?

_____

_____

5. What kind of education does Laura Park have?

_____

_____

6. Do any of the applicants know PASCAL?

_____

_____

7. What computer languages does Emma Singh know?

_____

_____

8. We need someone soon. Can any of the applicants start before the first?

_____

_____

9. Does Laura Park or Emma Singh have experience with mainframe computers?

_____

_____

10. Other than Tony, have any of these applicants applied here before?

_____

_____

You are an advisor at New World Alternative College. Below is a partial list of offered courses for the fall on the college's two campuses. Advise students of course offerings, using correlative conjunctions where possible.

English Composition	M	19:30-22:00	Philadelphia Campus
	TTh	9:30-11:00	Wilmington Campus
Technical Writing	MWF	13:00-14:00	Wilmington Campus
	TTh	19:00-20:30	Wilmington Campus
Linguistics	W	17:00-19:30	Wilmington Campus
	TTh	8:00-9:30	Philadelphia Campus
Philosophy	T	17:00-19:30	Wilmington Campus
	M	17:00-19:30	Philadelphia Campus
Economics	MWF	13:00-14:30	Philadelphia Campus
Anthropology	T	19:30-22:00	Wilmington Campus
Astronomy	Th	19:30-22:00	Wilmington Campus
	F	11:00-1:30	Wilmington Campus
Physics	W	19:30-22:00	Wilmington Campus

EXAMPLE: **Tom:** I need to take English composition and a social science course, but I can't drive to Wilmington.

Advisor: <u>You can take both English composition and economics at the Philadelphia campus.</u>

1.   **Lucy:** Can I complete my humanities requirements at the Wilmington campus?

Advisor: _____

_____

2.   **Tarek:** What can I take this fall to fulfill my social science requirement?

Advisor: _____

_____

3. **Leonore:** I can only come on Tuesdays and Thursdays during the daytime. Is there anything I can take this fall?

Advisor: _____

_____

4. **Ricardo:** I'm registered for philosophy right now. Is that the only course you offer on Tuesday nights?

Advisor: _____

_____

5.   **Abdul:** I'm registered for technical writing on Tuesday and Thursday nights, but my boss might move me to the night shift next week. Do you offer the course at any other time?

    Advisor: _____

_____

6.   **Tran:** When can I take astronomy?

    Advisor: _____

_____

7. **Li Hong:** Where can I take linguistics?

    Advisor: _____

_____

8.   **Jon:** I need to take a science course, but I work from 1:00 to 9:00 P.M. Do you have anything I can take?

    Advisor: _____

_____

9.   **Connie:** Can I take a humanities course at the Philadelphia campus?

    Advisor: _____

_____

10. **Moses:** I need a physical science course, but I work during the day. Do you have anything for me?

    Advisor: _____

_____

EXERCISE 4   (*Focus 3*)

Read each sentence. Write OK after sentences that are well-formed, parallel, and not repetitious. Rephrase the rest for concise, formal style.

EXAMPLE: Bridgeport won not only the game but also they won the league championship.

Bridgeport won not only the game but also the league championship.

1. Since I left my country, I have become more responsible and a more independent person.

_____

_____

2. In the fall, not only will I take accounting but also biology.

_____

_____

3. I both have been working very hard at my job and have been working very hard at school.

_____

_____

4. You either can come with us now or you can come with Lisa later.

_____

_____

5. Not only did Imelda get into the honors program, but also Nelson.

_____

_____

6. The board of directors decided both to open a Miami branch and to close the branches in Austin and Madison.

_____

_____

7. People from both the Middle East and Latin America attended the conference.

_____

_____

8. Marcus told me that either he would take his children to the museum or take them camping this weekend.

_____

_____

9. You will need to either present a driver's license or a major credit card to write a check in that store.

_____

_____

10. I know neither where Alma is nor what she is doing.

_____

_____

10. In Britain a truck is known as a lorry. In Australia it is called a ute.

_____

Complete the crossword puzzle.

ACROSS

2. _____ Paul nor Richard is likely to attend the barbecue on Saturday.
5. Elliott Richardson and George Mitchell, _____, were an attorney general and a senator.
7. We were _____ delighted and amazed at how many copies of our book sold.
8. To pay for Christie's tuition, they might _____ sell their vacation home or sell their stocks.

DOWN

1. The following sentence has a problem. It is not _____. When I return home this summer, I will both visit my parents and I will visit my relatives and friends.
3. The flight was _____ rough but also long.
4. They not only learned a few phrases of Mandarin but a few phrases of Korean _____.
6. The following sentence has a problem. It is not _____. Both swimming and to jog are what Martha likes to do after getting out of class.

UNIT

12 Sentence Connectors

EXERCISE 1   (*Focus 1*)

Complete the crossword puzzle.

ACROSS

2. _____ she exercised every day, she was never satisfied with the way she looked.
6. Sue Grafton always uses a letter of the alphabet in the title of her crime novels. For _____, K *is for Killer.*
8. You haven't paid the full amount this month on your loan. _____, next month you'll have to pay additional interest.
10. To access the Internet, you have to have a computer. _____, you need a modem.
11. I was extremely tired, _____ I kept studying.

DOWN

1. My uncle is quite generous. As a _____ of fact, he just gave $3,000 to an orphanage.
3. The Smiths' dog is usually well-behaved. _____, he did bite a mail carrier once.
4. Professor Reed is famous for giving low grades. In _____, nearly half of his students received only Cs last semester.
5. We might go to a movie tonight. On the other _____, we just might stay home and read.
7. _____ the moon rose, it was pitch dark in the forest.
9. In July the outdoors is predominantly green in the north, _____ in January everything is white.

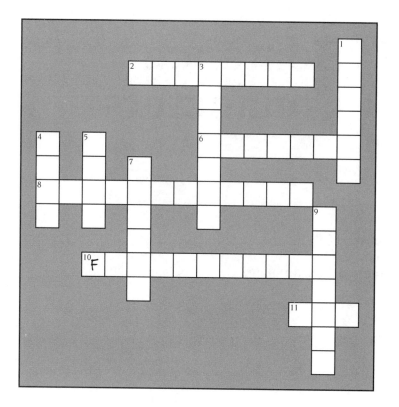

For each of the sentence pairs below, write down the relationship of the second sentence to the first: an added idea, an example, a similarity, a contrast (*used two times*), or a result.

EXAMPLE: Sigmund Freud found Greek myths to be useful in explaining psychological states. Carl Jung saw in Greek myths ways of explaining dreams.

Relationship: ____*a similarity*____

1. One of the most fascinating and compelling myths of the ancient Greeks was that of Persephone and Hades. Their story accounts for the seasons, the annual cycle of death and rebirth.

Relationship: _____

2. Hades was the god of the underworld, of darkness and stillness. His brother, Zeus, was the god of the sky and lord of storms.

Relationship: _____

3. Persephone was the daughter of Demeter, the goddess of fertility and agriculture. Like her mother, Persephone was associated with the ripening crops.

Relationship: _____

4. Hades was known as the "generous one" because he refused no one his hospitality, but he was also greedy and possessive. When he saw Persephone for the first time, he wanted her for himself.

    Relationship: _____

5. Because of Demeter's pleading with Zeus, Hades was not allowed to keep Persephone in his realm perpetually. He had to allow her to return to the surface of the earth for half of each year.

    Relationship: _____

6. Persephone rises in the spring and remains with her mother throughout the long, warm days of summer. In the fall, as the days get shorter and colder, she descends to Hades.

    Relationship: _____

EXERCISE 3   (Focus 2)

Use an appropriate connector from the list below to signal the addition relationship expressed in the last sentence of each pair or group of sentences. More than one connector may be appropriate for most contexts. Try to use a different connector in each sentence.

actually	as well	in addition	moreover
also	besides	in fact	what is more
as a matter of fact	furthermore		

EXAMPLE: California is particularly prone to earthquakes. In fact, I experienced one just last week while I was there on a short trip.

(Other possible connectors: all intensifying additive connectors)

1. Fiona loves learning alphabets and can read and write the Cyrillic. She has a grasp of Arabic, Hiragana, and Runes.

2. After Helen's operation, the doctor prescribed a potent antibiotic. She was given a painkiller.

3. I don't know how I'm going to manage to stay in shape this week with my crazy schedule. I've got a luncheon and dinner date every day of the week. I've even invited some people for tea tomorrow.

4. Nature is Patti's chief focus in life. When she's not working designing nature programs for children, she's out walking or sitting somewhere with binoculars or a magnifying glass.

5. Medical science has defeated many formerly fatal diseases. Smallpox has been eradicated. The incidences of tuberculosis and pneumonia have been greatly reduced or controlled.

6. The object of the game is to capture all of your opponent's pieces. You have to avoid capture by your opponent.

7. We could listen to classical music. We could listen to rock.

8. It was brilliantly clear last night. I could see all the individual stars of the Pleiades constellation. I could see stars that I had never seen before.

9. I'm afraid I can't go out tonight because I'm broke. I can't even pay the electric bill this month.

10. In a recent survey it was found that more than half of the patients sought alternative treatments such as massage, vitamins, and herbs. Some tried acupuncture, biofeedback, and meditation.

EXERCISE 4   (Focus 3)

Match each statement in column A with one in column B. Then rewrite them as one sentence using an alternative connector. Number 1 has been done for you as an example.

1. *I'm considering taking a course in medieval history next semester. On the other hand, I might enroll in a more practical course such as accounting.*

A	B
1. I'm considering taking a course in medieval history next semester.	a. Why don't you ask your well-off cousin in Dallas?
2. Bob and Sheila are thinking about celebrating their twenty-fifth anniversary with a weekend in New York City.	b. They could have done more to bring in tourists.
3. You already asked your sister for a loan.	c. They found that her use of historical data was often inaccurate.
4. The new Fords have a sleek, attractive design.	d. I might enroll in a more practical course such as accounting.
5. The city council announced a plan to attract businesses to the community.	e. We could plant a hedge.
6. We might put up a fence around our house.	f. Let's call up the theaters right now.
7. The critics praised the novelist for her thrilling plots and beautiful language.	g. Consider using thicker clothing and wearing a net around your head.
8. To keep the insects away, spray this repellent all over your body and clothes.	h. They might take the whole family on a week-long beach holiday in Maine.
9. I guess I should have my old camera repaired.	i. The Toyotas get better gas mileage.
10. Let's get a newspaper on the way home and check the movie listings for this evening.	j. Maybe I should buy a new one and get something more reliable.

2. _____

_____

3. _____

_____

4. _____

_____

5. _____

_____

6. _____

_____

7. _____

_____

8. _____

_____

9. _____

_____

10. _____

_____

EXERCISE 5   (Focus 4)

Use an exemplifying, identifying, or clarifying connector from the list below that would be appropriate for each blank. Use each only one time.

for example	to illustrate	that is	namely
for instance	in particular	in other words	specifically

1. Commerce has never been shy to borrow and profit from classical myths. **(a)** _____, we have Mercury automobiles, Midas mufflers, Ajax detergent, Zephyr and Bellerophon books, and Electra records, to name but a few. Mobil gas stations, **(b)** _____, fly the banner of the winged horse, Pegasus.

2. The critics found the book tedious, sloppy, and juvenile; _____, they detested it.

3. Medicine has borrowed heavily from Greek and Latin. Psychology, _____, with names such as the _Oedipus complex_ to describe primal inner drives, owes a major debt to the ancients.

4. There is one thing you can do before you leave; _____, you can make sure that all the documents we worked on today have been backed up.

5. Greek and Roman place names crop up everywhere in the eastern United States. Just glance at a map of New York State, _____. There we find the towns of Troy, Ithaca, Rome, Carthage, and Corinth, among others.

6. You should never make anyone lose face; _____, you shouldn't do or say anything that will embarrass them in front of anyone else.

7. I don't understand the part about business expenses on the new tax form. _____, how does line *h* on page 2 relate to line *q* on page 4?

EXERCISE 6   (*Focus 5*)

In the sentence pairs below, the second sentence is repetitious. Rephrase or condense the information in these sentences and add a similarity sentence connector.

EXAMPLE: To gain the status of hero, Theseus conquered the Minotaur. Perseus conquered Medusa to gain the status of hero.

REVISED: <u>Likewise, Perseus killed Medusa to become a hero.</u>

1. Among some of the people of the Pacific, there is an attitude that a person belongs to a specific piece of land even if he or she leaves home for a long period. Among the Greeks, there is an attitude that a person belongs to a specific piece of land even if he or she leaves home for a long period.

_____

_____

2. In the Middle East it is taboo to eat with your left hand. In India it is taboo to eat with your left hand.

_____

_____

3. Prem shows that he is environmentally conscious by taking public transportation or riding his bicycle whenever he can. Suraiya shows that she is environmentally aware by recycling paper products and by composting organic matter instead of just throwing things in the trash.

_____

_____

4. T-cells help to maintain a healthy body by destroying abnormal cells before they proliferate. B-cells help to maintain a healthy body by manufacturing antibodies.

_____

_____

5. Bonaventure Island, off the tip of Quebec's Gaspé Peninsula, is the site of a spectacular seabird colony during summer. The Klamath Basin in California is the site of a spectacular waterfowl concentration during autumn.

_____

_____

EXERCISE 7   (Focus 5)

The chart on page 116 gives information about some commonly used herbs. Imagine that you are a student investigating medicinal herbs, and that you have been asked to write a summary of the ways in which these herbs are similar. As preparation for your summary, use the information in the chart to make at least five pairs of sentences expressing similarity. Use a similarity connector with the second sentence of each pair.

EXAMPLE: Ginger promotes circulation; cayenne likewise aids this important
          bodily function.

1. _____

_____

2. _____

_____

3. _____

_____

4. _____

_____

5. _____

_____

EXERCISE 8   (Focus 6)

Use the information in the chart from Exercise 7 to make up five sentence pairs expressing differences between the herbs, their uses, and preparation.

EXAMPLE: Cayenne is a stimulant. Chamomile, on the other hand, is a sedative.

1. _____

_____

2. _____

_____

Name of Herb	Ginger	Dandelion	Chamomile	Echinachea	Cayenne
Part Used	root	root or leaf	flower	root	fruit
Systems Affected	stomach, intestines, circulation	liver, kidneys, gallbladder, pancreas	nerves, stomach, kidneys, liver	blood, lymph	stomach, heart, circulation, blood, respiratory
Properties/ Actions	stimulant, antigas, induces sweating	diuretic, laxative, tonic	nervine, tonic, induces sweating, sedative, antigas	blood purifier, anti-microbial, antiseptic	stimulant, antigas, antispasmodic, antiseptic, tonic, blood purifier
Indications	promotes circulation, relieves fever, supports digestion	stimulates kidneys, reduces inflammation, relieves congestion of liver & gallbladder & rheumatic pain	general calming action for restlessness, nervous stomach, & insomnia, relieves inflammation in mouth, throat, & eyes, supports digestion	helps rid body of infections, restores proper bodily functions, increases health & vitality	promotes circulation, supports digestion, relieves colds, headaches, & rheumatic pain, strengthens heart, relieves throat ailments
Preparation and Dosage	Pour a cup of boiling water onto 1 teaspoon of fresh root and let infuse for 5 minutes. Drink whenever needed.	Put 2–3 teaspoons of root into one cup of water, bring to a boil, and simmer 10–15 minutes. Drink 3x daily. Leaves may be eaten raw in salad.	Pour a cup of boiling water onto 2 teaspoons of flowers & let infuse 5–10 minutes. For throat, decoct half a cup of flowers in 2 liters water. Allow to cool.	Put 1–2 teaspoons of root in 1 cup of water and bring to a boil slowly, simmer for 10–15 minutes. Drink 3x daily.	Pour a cup of boiling water onto 1/2–1 teaspoon & let infuse 10 minutes. A tablespoon of the infusion should be mixed with hot water and drunk whenever needed.

(Information from David Hoffman, *The Holistic Herbal*, Findhorn, Moray, Scotland: The Findhorn Press, 1985, and Michael Tierra, *The Way of Herbs*, New York: Washington Square Press, 1983.)

3. _____

_____

4. _____

_____

5. _____

_____

EXERCISE 7 (*Focus 7*)

Some of the following sentences contain the wrong sentence connector. Find any errors and correct them.

1. Judy got As in English, French, and history. She didn't do so well, nevertheless, in chemistry.

_____

_____

2. The new Jeep is said to be environmentally friendly because its air-conditioning system does not use CFCs. In fact, it doesn't get very good gas mileage.

_____

_____

3. She thought everybody would laugh at her new hairstyle. Even so, hardly anyone noticed.

_____

_____

4. I think that Hamid is probably at home right now. On the other hand, he might still be in transit.

_____

_____

5. Chen didn't have a lot of money. In contrast, he made contributions to local charities.

_____

_____

6. Parsley is a very flavorful and useful kitchen herb. In fact, it's excellent for the digestion.

_____

_____

The chart below gives information about individual achievements that involved overcoming certain difficulties. Use the information to make up sentence pairs linked by a concession connector. Use a variety of connectors. The choice of subject nouns or pronouns is up to you, as is any other information you wish to add.

EXAMPLE: *The expedition encountered blizzards, extreme cold, and*
avalanches. Nevertheless, they reached the top of Mount Everest.

DIFFICULTY	ACHIEVEMENT
1. blizzards, extreme cold, avalanches	reached the top of Mount Everest
2. lost parents at an early age	became renowned diplomat
3. addicted to alcohol and drugs	kicked the habits and became a better musician
4. settling into a new community	new friends and sense of inner strength
5. car breakdowns	got across the country

1. _____

   _____

2. _____

   _____

3. _____

   _____

4. _____

   _____

5. _____

   _____

The two charts following give information about various characters from history, myths, and legends. Use the information from Chart A to make sentence pairs expressing reason-result relationships. Use Chart B to make sentence pairs expressing purpose relationships. For all sentence pairs, use an appropriate sentence connector.

EXAMPLE: *Ariadne, the daughter of King Minos of Crete, gave Theseus a ball of thread. As a result, he was able to find his way out of the labyrinth after slaying the Minotaur.*

CHART A

CHARACTER(S)	EVENT/SITUATION	RESULT
1. Ariadne, daughter of King Minos of Crete	gave Theseus a ball of thread	find his way out of the labyrinth after slaying the Minotaur
2. King Henry VIII of England	wanted a male heir	divorced his first wife
3. Adam and Eve	ate the forbidden fruit	were cast out of the garden of Eden
4. Tristan and Iseult	drank the love potion intended for King Mark and Iseult	they fell deeply and tragically in love
5. Inanna, Sumerian sky goddess	descended into the underworld and underwent death	bring her beloved husband back to life

1. _____

_____

2. _____

_____

3. _____

_____

4. _____

_____

5. _____

_____

CHART B

CHARACTER(S)	ACTION/EVENT	PURPOSE
1. The Aztecs	sacrificed prisoners of war	keep the sun in motion and increase the bounty of nature.
2. Ulysses	had his men plug their ears and had himself roped securely to the mast of his ship	hear the song of the sirens and survive
3. James Bond	risked his life	save the world from megalomaniacs
4. Johnny Appleseed	sowed seeds wherever he went	spread apple trees around the United States

1. _____

_____

2. _____

_____

3. _____

_____

4. _____

_____

EXERCISE 12 (Focus 8)

Provide the correct punctuation of the connectors in the sentences below if needed.

EXAMPLE: Heracles was much admired by the gods however he was despised by Hera.

Heracles was much admired by the gods; however, he was despised by Hera.

1. Ancient Egyptians saw the earth as an egg guarded at night by the moon, a great white bird. Similarly the early Christian gnostics saw heaven and earth as a world egg around which coiled a giant serpent.

_____

_____

2. The study of geography owes a lot to Ptolemy who lived just less than two thousand years ago. The grid system which he adopted and improved remains in fact the basis of modern cartography.

_____

_____

3. Ptolemy drew upon the works of Strabo, another ancient geographer. Strabo was also an historian and one of the great travelers of his day.

_____

_____

4. Ptolemy's influence was considerable however he made some significant miscalculations.

_____

_____

5. Ptolemy prepared Europe for world exploration though having rejected the notion of the earth as a disk surrounded by the river Oceanus.

_____

_____

6. Spiders are a very misunderstood group of arthropods. For example when people see spiders, some feel disgust, while some try to kill them, and some scream and run away.

_____

_____

7. Spiders are often feared by people. They are also much maligned.

_____

_____

8. Most spiders are actually very helpful. The most important predators of insects in the world, spiders protect plants for instance by eliminating many harmful insects.

_____

_____

TOEFL®

Test Preparation Exercises
Units 10–12

Choose the *one* word or phrase that best completes each sentence.

1. The coaches admired _____ the new player defended the goal.
   - (A) how
   - (B) the way how
   - (C) that
   - (D) in which

2. Students at State College can choose from a wide variety of majors; _____, there are degree programs in nursing, computer science, humanities, and agriculture.
   - (A) moreover
   - (B) besides that
   - (C) for example
   - (D) similarly

3. Toronto is the city _____.
   - (A) which my sister moved
   - (B) my sister moved to
   - (C) my sister moved to it
   - (D) to that my sister moved

4. Fred bought the car stripped; _____, he bought it with no frills such as a radio or an air conditioner.
   - (A) furthermore
   - (B) for example
   - (C) in other words
   - (D) especially

5. The period from the fourteenth to the seventeenth centuries, _____ the arts of ancient Greece were studied again in Europe, is known as the Renaissance.
   - (A) was when
   - (B) who
   - (C) when
   - (D) where

6. Naguib and Ahmed are a doctor and an architect, respectively. _____.
   - (A) They can help you design your house.
   - (B) Naguib can help you design your house.
   - (C) Ahmed can help you design your house.
   - (D) It is impressive that each man could have two degrees.

7. Not only _____, she also set a new record.
   - (A) Sabrina won the race
   - (B) Sabrina did win the race
   - (C) did Sabrina win the race
   - (D) Sabrina wins the race

8. We _____ Rome nor Florence; instead, we spent most of our time in Venice.
   - (A) didn't see neither
   - (B) did see neither
   - (C) neither saw
   - (D) saw neither

9. It's not at all certain what Gloria will do this summer. She might work as a volunteer. _____, she might take extra courses so that she can get her degree earlier.
   (A) Similarly
   (B) On the other hand
   (C) Either
   (D) Instead of

10. _____ Jonathan was able to get the facts faster than anyone else in the class was because he had mastered the art of searching on the Internet.
   (A) The way
   (B) The place where
   (C) As a result
   (D) The reason

Identify the *one* underlined word or phrase that must be changed for the sentence to be grammatically correct.

11. Nonnative plant species have taken a major hold in this country. <u>In fact</u>, in the last ten
    A
    years, more habitat has probably been lost to exotic plants than to development.
    <u>Alien plants, i.e.,</u> Scotch and French broom, pampas grass, ice plant, and eucalyptus, are
    B
    prolific in California. <u>Likewise</u>, kudzu is so widespread in the southern states <u>that it is</u>
    C   **D**
    <u>known as</u> the vine that ate the south.

12. <u>The place to where you go</u> in London <u>when you want</u> a map of <u>anywhere in the world</u> is
    A   **B**   **C**
    Stanford's. It's on Longacre, not far from Covent Garden, <u>which is</u> quite a tourist mecca
                                                              D
    these days.

13. The 1980s were a spectacular decade for Wayne Gretzky, the star hockey player with the
    Edmonton Oilers. <u>From 1981 to 1987 consecutively</u>, he was the NHL's leading scorer and
                     A
    winner of the Ross trophy. <u>And every year from</u> 1980 to 1987, <u>however</u>, he was the NHL's
                               B   **C**
    MVP and winner of the Hart Memorial trophy. <u>In addition to</u> these trophies and
                                                D
    distinctions, Gretzky won several other awards and became a highly paid celebrity.

14. They never explained <u>the reason for why</u> they were searching the train, but we had to
                         A
    show our passports and then open our luggage, <u>which they went through</u> with
                                                  B
    embarrassingly keen interest. It was the middle of the night <u>when this occurred</u> and we
                                                                 C
    had to get off the train and wait on a platform <u>that was dingy and cold</u> for one hour
                                                    D
    before they allowed us to get back on.

15. Natalie didn't think she would have enough energy to go to the concert tonight. <u>Not only</u>
A
<u>she had stayed up</u> half the night working on her thesis, <u>but she also did</u> some volunteer
B
work in the morning <u>and jogged</u> in the afternoon. She is <u>both</u> tired and deserving of rest.
C **D**

16. We often have a hard time in our family deciding where to go together for vacation. Last
summer, <u>for example</u>, my mother wanted to go to the Aegean. My father, <u>on the other</u>
A **B**
<u>hand</u>, insisted that he needed a dose of cold weather. The high Himalayas or the Andes
<u>were his alternatives</u>. My sister wanted to visit Japan, and I had my heart set on the
C
Australian outback. <u>Nevertheless</u>, we all went our separate ways.
D

17. <u>Both</u> Peter Paul Rubens and Anthony Trollope were men of many talents. Rubens was
A
<u>both</u> a painter and a diplomat, <u>respectively</u>, while Trollope was a doctor <u>as well as</u> a
B **C** **D**
novelist.

18. Rick: Do <u>either</u> of you have to take French or Spanish this semester?
A

Sandy: <u>Neither</u>. I've finished my language requirement.
B

Liz: I'm not sure yet. I think I'll take <u>both</u> Russian or Chinese.
C

Rick: Good luck. <u>Not only are those languages</u> complex but they have different alphabets
D
too.

19. <u>The reason they hired</u> that construction firm to build the addition to their house
A
<u>was because</u> they admired <u>the way how they worked</u>, that is, their efficiency, their speed,
B **C**
<u>and above all</u>, their attention to details.
D

20. Andrea's vacation was a disaster <u>likewise</u>. <u>In addition to</u> losing her glasses, she twisted
A **B**
her ankle and spent most of her sight-seeing time limping around in pain. <u>Besides that</u>,
C
someone stole her passport and it rained nearly every day. <u>Despite all of this</u>, she met
D
some very kind and helpful people.

UNIT 13 Modal Perfect Verbs

PART A

Carol and Dave decided to stop seeing each other. Both of them have been thinking about the reasons their relationship went bad. Fill in each blank with the active voice of the modal perfect verb given.

EXAMPLE: Carol wonders if she ___could have treated___ (could, treat) Dave better.

Carol thinks she **(1)** _____ (could, be) nicer to Dave when he forgot her birthday; Dave thinks he often **(2)** _____ (may, spend) too much time with his friends instead of with Carol. Carol feels that she **(3)** _____ (should, not expect) Dave to know how hurt she was about the birthday incident without telling him; Dave knows that he **(4)** _____ (should, not hang up) the phone on Carol when they got into their last argument. Both of them feel that they **(5)** _____ (could, do) a lot of things differently to improve their relationship.

PART B

Fill in each blank with the passive form of the modal given.

EXAMPLE: Dave knows that some things ___should have been left___ (should, leave) unsaid.

Carol's brother agreed that their last argument **(6)** _____ (could, handle) better; Dave's sister insisted that she **(7)** _____ (should, told) about the problems they were having. Carol feels that there **(8)** _____ (might, not be) so many problems between them if they had only talked more; Dave feels that there were a lot of things that **(9)** _____ (should, not say). Both of them feel that their problems **(10)** _____ (could, avoid) if they had seen them more clearly.

PART C

Fill in the blanks with the modal perfect and present participle form of the verb given.

EXAMPLE: Carol thinks that Dave ____ _must have been dreaming_ ____
(must, dream) when he asked if they could still be friends.

Carol wonders what she **(11)** _____ (must, think) when she told Dave she hated him. Dave wonders what on earth he **(12)** _____ (could, hope for) when he tried to make things better by calling Carol to talk at 2 A.M. Both of them feel that they **(13)** _____ (should, pay) more attention to each other instead of worrying about other things.

EXERCISE 2   (*Focus 2*)

In your textbook, review the meanings expressed by the modals *should have*, *could have*, and *might have*. In the exercise below, underline the word(s) in each sentence that provide a clue to help you choose the best modal. Then fill in the blank with the appropriate modal. Some blanks have more than one possible answer.

EXAMPLE: I <u>regret</u> that I yelled at you. I ____ _should have been_ ____ nicer.

Carol was really irritated when Dave said that their problems were all her fault. She felt that he **(1)** _____ (accept) some of the blame.

Dave felt that Carol **(2)** _____ (do) a lot to help a friend of his who worked with her. It was well within her abilities as office manager to prevent him from getting laid off.

Carol believed it was really thoughtless of Dave to volunteer to work overtime on Christmas Eve. He **(3)** _____ (work) overtime almost any other night of the year.

Dave told Carol that he really regretted some of his actions, and that he **(4)** _____ (be) more thoughtful.

Carol was really angry at Dave when he showed up an hour late for a dinner date. She felt that at least he **(5)** _____ (call).

Dave thought that Carol made a really rude comment to his sister about her prom dress. Carol **(6)** _____ (have) the decency to keep her negative thoughts to herself.

Despite being aware that Dave had an exam the next week, Carol felt that he was perfectly able to come to help her move into her new apartment, and that he **(7)** _____ (help) with some of the heavy items.

Dave strongly criticized Carol for saying that she wasn't feeling well one evening when she later went out with friends. She **(8)** _____ (tell) him the truth.

Carol reproached Dave for the same offense, saying that he **(9)** _____ (remember) the time that he had said he had to work overtime, but went fishing instead.

Both of them know that they did some pretty thoughtless things, and that they **(10)** _____ (think) before they acted.

■ EXERCISE 3 ■ (*Focus 3*)

Betty and Elizabeth are housemates. Betty is always informal whereas Elizabeth is always formal. Fill in the blanks in their conversation below with the correct form of either *be supposed to have* **or** *be to have.*

Elizabeth: You know that we **(1)** _____ finished our group projects by next Tuesday. The instructor expects to have them graded by Thursday.

Betty: I thought we **(2)** _____ turned them in by last Friday. Oh well, I didn't turn in anything, anyway.

Elizabeth: Our bibliographies **(3)** _____ turned in by then. Don't you remember?

Betty: I guess I forgot. When **(4)** _____ completed our term papers? By the end of the semester?

Elizabeth: No, silly. We **(5)** _____ them done two weeks before the end. You'd better get busy!

Betty: By the way, **(6)** _____ paid this month's rent last Friday?

Elizabeth: Betty, you poor thing. You're all confused. We **(7)** _____ paid it by this coming Friday. Do you have your share?

Betty: I hope I will. My parents **(8)** _____ send me a check soon.

PART A

Fill in the blanks with *must have*, *can't have*, *should have*, or *would have*.

Mahmoud: Uh-oh, the clock on the wall in the computer lab is four hours behind. The power **(1)** _____ gone off during the night.

Najat: Oh, dear. I hope our project wasn't lost. Hakim was working on it last night. He's fairly reliable. He **(2)** _____ made backup copies while he was working. Let's check the directory and see.

Mahmoud: There's nothing here. The power **(3)** _____ gone off before he backed anything up.

Najat: Wait a minute—that **(4)** _____ happened! Hakim **(5)** _____ left a note if something had gone wrong while he was here. He always finishes exactly at 3 and the clock says 11:10 now so the power **(6)** _____ gone off after he left.

PART B

The following is an excerpt from the script of a cowboy movie. One group is waiting to ambush another group. Fill in the blanks with *must have*, *can't have*, *should have*, *would have*, or *wouldn't have*.

First Cowboy: Well, where are they? We've been waiting here more than two hours. They **(7)** _____ been here by now.

Second Cowboy: Someone **(8)** _____ tipped them off. Do you think it was one of our bunch?

First Cowboy: Impossible. It **(9)** _____ been one of ours. They're all tried and true.

Second Cowboy: What about our latest member—that young Billy?

First Cowboy: No, it **(10)** _____ been him. We didn't tell him anything about this. He **(11)** _____ known.

One of the tasks of an attorney in court is to weaken opposing witnesses' testimony by inducing uncertainty wherever possible. One way to do this is by asking questions expressing uncertainty or possibility, as opposed to certainty. Read the dialogue below and write in the missing questions. The first one has been done for you as an example.

Attorney: On the night of the murder, did you see my client enter room 132 of the Tropicana Motel?

Witness: Yes, I did. I was sitting on a bench on the sidewalk when I saw a tall, thin man go into one of the rooms.

Attorney: (1) _Could it have been someone else_____?

Witness: Oh, no; the person was definitely your client.

Attorney: (2) _____?

Witness: Definitely not. Nobody else looks like your client. I recognized his mustache and hat.

Attorney: (3) _____?

Witness: It may have been. There are a lot of doors on that side of the building. But I went back the next day to check, after I read about the murder in the newspaper.

Attorney: (4) _____?

Witness: No, I don't think so. I clearly remember the location of the door. I just wasn't sure of the number of the door.

Attorney: Do you remember exactly what time it was?

Witness: Yes. The sun had gone down just a little while before I saw your client, so it was 7:00.

Attorney: (5) _____?

Witness: I guess it could have been later, but not much later.

Attorney: Why were you sitting there anyway?

Witness: I was just killing time.

Attorney: (6) _____?

Witness: Well, I had a little bit of wine with me, but it wasn't much.

Attorney: (7) _____?

Witness: That depends—how much is a lot?

Attorney: There was a nearly empty bottle of wine beside the bench you were sitting on.

Witness: Well, that's not a lot for me. I can drink much more than that.

Attorney: (8) _____?

Witness: Well, I've been in some treatment programs, but I wouldn't call myself an alcoholic.

Attorney: (9) _____?

Witness: Okay, so I may have been a little drunk. I still remember everything clearly.

Attorney: Thank you. That will be all.

Each numbered group of statements below expresses certainty about the cause of a situation. For each, give an alternative explanation, using a perfective modal that expresses possibility. An example is given for the first one. Can you think of any others?

1. My computer's not working. Joe was using it yesterday. He must have done something to it.

   Alternate explanation: ___The fuse in the power cord may have blown.___

2. Look! Isn't that our cat that just ran into the bushes? I could've sworn I locked him in the house.

   Alternate explanation:_____

   _____

3. I left my briefcase here on this table and now it's gone. Somebody must have stolen it.

   Alternate explanation:_____

   _____

4. My shirt doesn't fit anymore. It must have shrunk in the wash.

   Alternate explanation:_____

   _____

5. Ramon is driving an expensive new car. He must have won the lottery.

   Alternate explanation:_____

   _____

6. The Joneses didn't send us a Christmas card. They must not care about us any more.

   Alternate explanation:_____

   _____

Larry is angry at his son's choice of clothing for a job interview. Larry's wife Connie feels that Larry is being too hard on the boy, and that a lot of the outcomes he predicts are not certain. Using the modals *would have*, *could have*, and *might have*, make Larry's predictions as certain as possible, and Connie's less certain and more polite. The first two have been done for you as examples.

Larry: I can't believe he didn't get a haircut before the interview! If he had gotten a nice crew cut like mine, he **(1)** __would have_____ gotten that job!

Connie: Now, dear, you never know. Crew cuts aren't as stylish these days. The boss **(2)** __might have_____ felt the boy's hair was fine.

Larry: And his clothes! What possessed him to wear those outlandish clothes to a job interview? If he had worn that suit I gave him he **(3)** _____ gotten more respect. I did when I wore it to my first interview.

Connie: If he had worn your ancient suit, the boss **(4)**_____ thought he'd stepped out of a time machine!

Larry: And he **(5)** _____ been impressed! My boss was!

Connie: You **(6)** _____ forgotten a few details, dear. I recall that it took you a half dozen interviews before you got your first job.

Larry: But the point is that I got it—just like our son **(7)** _____ if he had only dressed respectably.

Connie: Honey, the boss **(8)** _____ actually looked at our son's credentials instead of just his clothes. He has an excellent education, you know. And you shouldn't be so sure that he didn't get the job—he **(9)** _____. Didn't they say they would call him within a week?

Larry: They **(10)** _____ called by now if he had gotten the job.

Connie: They **(11)** _____ had a hard time deciding. There were a lot of other candidates for the job.

(*Telephone rings; Connie answers it and sounds excited.*)

Connie: You **(12)** _____ been a little more tolerant of your son. That was his new boss calling—he got the job!

Larry: Oh, really? Well, that's my boy, a chip off the old block! You know, dear, it is slightly possible that I **(13)** _____ been just a little bit wrong this time.

EXERCISE 8   (*Focus 7*)

Use the information in the first and second columns to express what will most likely have happened by the time period in the third column. You may want to add an *if* or *unless* clause to your sentence to qualify your statement.

EXAMPLE: June   the workers will be on strike   December

By December the workers will have been on strike for six months.

8:00 A.M.	I will be working	8:00 P.M.

_____

1900	the Anderson family own their farm	2000

January	Jason, at 260 pounds, promises to lose 10 pounds per month	June

_____

_____

present	the club shall elect its first president for a two-year term	two years from now
1997	Hong Kong becomes a part of China	2007
1998	Lisa begins work on her bachelor's degree	2003

EXERCISE 9 (Focus 8)

Solve the crossword puzzle found on page 134.

ACROSS

1. You _____ have ignored that remark she made. I don't know why you didn't.
3. They surely _____ have given you a ride if they'd known you needed one.
4. You were _____ deposited the check yesterday. Why didn't you?
5. By this time next month we will _____ 300 miles of our projected hike along the Pacific Crest Trail.
6. I _____ left my umbrella in the library. It was one of the places I went after the rain stopped.
7. I shouldn't have listened to her advice means I _____ having listened to her advice.
9. The speaker is expressing _____ in the following sentences. "Why did you pick up the phone? You could've just let it ring."
10. You were _____ to have had your car inspected last month.

DOWN

1. The statement "Abraham Lincoln would not have approved of the debate" is actually _____ to fact.
2. Look at that woman with the braids and all the make-up and nail polish. She _____ spent hours doing that.
6. I _____ have been playing with the New York Philharmonic Orchestra if only I had practiced more.
8. I _____ have filled the tank up at the last station. Now I've run out of gas in the middle of the desert

UNIT 14 Discourse Organizers

Solve the crossword puzzle.

ACROSS

2. We have examined some of the prevalent theories concerning the origin of diseases. _____, let's move on to the topic of how diseases are spread.

5. "Isn't the quality of the air we breathe of any concern to the average person today?" This sentence is an example of a _____ question.

7. "Overall," "briefly," and "in short" are examples of _____ connectors.

9. Words such as "second," "third," "after that," and "lastly" are used to show the _____ of topics, points, and events.

DOWN

   1. *There + be* is often used to _____ a topic.
   3. _____ we have spent three hours discussing the issues. Now, how are we going to solve our most pressing problems?
4 & 8. My talk will cover three main areas. (4) _____, the importance of rivers from a geographical perspective. Second, the importance of rivers on human history, and (8) _____, the evolution of ports and port cities.
   6. _____ several things you need to know before you buy a computer.

EXERCISE 2   (Focus 2)

Fill in each blank by choosing the correct sequential connector.

1. Looking at the whole book, we can certainly see that the main characters had their share of mishaps on their journey, but, _____, everything worked out for the better.
   (a) in the end   **(b)** in conclusion

2. _____, allow me to reiterate — the surest way to prevent burglary is to install a home security system.
   (a) In the end   **(b)** To conclude

3. **(A)** _____ we thought that the mysterious cloud that lingered on the horizon all throughout the day was simply the product of wind and dust.
   (B) _____ we found that the assumption was not the case.
   (A)   **(a)** At first   **(b)** The first
   (B)   **(a)** Later   **(b)** Next

4. To make pancakes, _____ preheat the oven to 400° F.
   (a) at first   **(b)** first

5. My old car broke down five times in January. _____, I had no choice but to replace it.
   (a) Subsequently   **(b)** Next

6. The _____ most common tax error is using the wrong tax table.
   (a) secondly   **(b)** second

7. Our _____ word of warning is not to consume alcoholic beverages if you are taking this medication.
   (a) at last   **(b)** final

Make up a sentence with a beginning sequential connector that could follow each of the sentences below. Try to use a variety of connectors.

EXAMPLE: Money is always a problem. *To start with, I never seem to have enough of it.*

1. Money is always a problem.

2. Building a house involves many different activities.

3. When I was a child I had several daily chores.

4. To make a pot of tea, follow these steps.

5. I can make some recommendations about how to learn a language.

6. Bringing up a child is no simple task.

7. Today, stress is a fact of life.

EXERCISE 4 (*Focus 2*)

For the sentences below, write a list of ideas that could follow, using beginning, continuation, and concluding sequential connectors in your list. Try to use a variety of connectors.

EXAMPLE: If I won the lottery and became a millionaire, I would be overjoyed. *First of all, I'd throw a big party. Next, I'd find a beautiful place to live. Finally, I'd take a long vacation and travel around the world.*

1. If I won the lottery and become a millionaire, I would be overjoyed.

2. Writing a research paper is hard work.

_____

_____

3. Summer is a great time.

_____

_____

4. Staying in good shape takes commitment.

_____

_____

5. To keep my car running smoothly, I do some important things.

_____

_____

6. Reading is one of the best ways of improving your language.

_____

_____

7. Sleep is wonderful.

_____

_____

8. A good husband (wife or companion) has the following characteristics.

_____

_____

EXERCISE 5 (Focus 3)

Fill in the blanks with appropriate words or phrases. Use different forms of connectors for each passage. Add commas where needed.

1. _____ two basic _____ of spiders. _____ are web builders. _____ are wandering spiders.

2. _____ three major _____ of rocks, classified into groups determined by how they were formed. _____ is igneous rock, which crystallizes from molten magma or lava. _____ is sedimentary rock, which forms in layers or strata and often has fossils. And _____ is metamorphic rock, which has been changed considerably from its original igneous or sedimentary structure and composition.

3. _____ several significant _____ in which Marx went beyond the philosophy of history of his day. _____, the activity of human working populations was more important to him than philosophical abstractions. _____, he replaced a closed system of speculation with a critical philosophy that attempted to unify theory and practice. _____, he asked revolutionary questions, such as what constitutes the alienation of labor. _____, he turned his history of human labor into a criticism of labor in society.

(Information from Kevin Reilly, *The West and the World, A Topical History of Civilization*, New York: Harper & Row, 1980.)

4. _____ a few _____ regarding the extinction of the dinosaurs. _____, and perhaps the most popular, is that the earth was hit by a meteor, and the dust from the impact blocked out the light necessary to maintain adequate plant life. _____ theory holds that rather than something coming from outer space, there was a gigantic volcanic explosion that threw huge quantities of dust into the atmosphere. _____ , _____ the more farfetched explanations such as the expansion of the swift and stealthy mammal population, which had developed a great appetite for dinosaur eggs.

5. _____ four remarkable _____ about the universe that encourage us to investigate whether we are alone. _____ is that space is transparent. A ray of starlight can speed unimpeded through space for thousands of millions of years. _____, the universe is uniform. Wherever we look, everything appears to be built out of the same chemical elements we find at home. _____, the universe is isotropic, which is to say that on the large scale it looks pretty much the same in every direction—every observer sees galaxies stretching off into all parts of the sky, just as we do. _____, the universe is abundant. Within the range of our telescopes lie perhaps one hundred billion galaxies, each home to a hundred billion or so stars. From such considerations has arisen the endeavor called SETI—the search for intelligent life in the universe.

[NOTE: SETI = search for extraterrestrial intelligence]

(From Timothy Ferris, *The Mind's Sky, Human Intelligence in a Cosmic Context*. New York: Bantam Books, 1992.)

Write a summary statement for each of the sentences or brief passages below, using the summary connector indicated in parentheses. For statements that introduce topics, make up a sentence that fits the context.

EXAMPLE: This report will examine the impact of the arms industry on the increasing violence in the world. (briefly)

Briefly, there is a strong link between the arms industry and the rising tide of violence in the world.

1. My presentation will focus on the effects on the globe of greenhouse gases. (briefly)

   _____

   _____

2. Ladies and gentlemen of the jury: We have heard here today the testimony of expert witnesses. It is now well established that my client was miles from the scene of the crime when the events in question took place. What is more, the weapon found in the glove compartment of my client's car could not have fired the bullet found lodged in the door at 76 Ocean Boulevard. (in short)

   _____

   _____

3. The consensus has too often been that the 1950s were a dull decade characterized by bland mediocrity and timid conformity. Recent books, however, have begun to alter our perceptions of this misunderstood period. When we look closely at the canvases of Pollock and de Kooning, when we listen carefully to the music of Miles Davis, the poetry of the Beats, and the voices of the burgeoning movements for social justice, we recognize passion and creativity, not caution. (all in all)

   _____

   _____

4. So far, I have examined some prevalent ideas about lung cancer. (as has been previously mentioned)

   _____

   _____

5. Biological diversity is the key to mankind's survival. Only by conserving the vast variety of plant and animal life, using and sharing it wisely, can we hope to feed everyone adequately and meet future challenges of a rapidly changing world. (in summary)

   _____

   _____

6. Our company has never had a better year. Our stock has made gains consistently throughout every quarter. We've more than doubled our profits over those of last year. We've added five hundred new employees to our payroll, and on the drawing board are plans for a new production plant. (overall)

_____

_____

7. These are a few health tips to take into consideration when visiting Nepal. Watching what you eat or drink while in Kathmandu and on the trail is critical. Tap water and river water are strictly off limits unless boiled briskly for at least 20 minutes. Some people have successfully used water filters. Raw fruits and vegetables should be avoided unless they've been completely peeled. (in summary)

_____

_____

8. The lifesaving benefits of automotive air bag systems are well known. What isn't well known is that many components, including the bag itself, are made of plastic. Plastic makes a lot of things safe. For example, plastic packaging keeps medical equipment sterile and harmful medicines out of the hands of children. Plastic wraps and trays keep food fresh and safe. And shatter-resistant plastic bottles have prevented thousands of accidents. (briefly)

_____

_____

EXERCISE 7   (Focus 5)

The excerpts below are from the beginning paragraphs of books, articles, or essays. For each, predict what the rest of the text might be about.

1. Why should there be such an extraordinary variety of animals all doing the same things? Why should a whale have warm blood and lungs, whereas a similarly sized swimming monster, the whale shark, has cold blood and gills? Why do indigenous Australian mammals rear their young in a pouch whereas mammals in the northern hemisphere retain their offspring within a womb and nourish them by means of a placenta?

_____

_____

2. Does it take you more than ten minutes to find a particular letter, bill, report, or other paper from your files (or piles of paper on your desk)? Are there papers on your desk, other than reference materials, that you haven't looked through for a week or more? Do magazines and newspapers pile up unread? Do you frequently procrastinate so long on a work assignment that it becomes an emergency or panic situation?

_____

_____

3. How many times have you thought about giving money to a cause, but you can't find one that addresses more than one issue? Is there a way to ensure your donations affect both

cultural and environmental preservation?

_____

_____

4. Thinking about buying a computer that the whole family can use? How will it serve everyone using it? Is it for entertainment, education, tracking family finances, running a small business, or all of the above?

_____

_____

5. Do we want to wait five minutes or more every time we have to cross the street? Does every green space have to be filled with a house or a shop? Do we all have to breathe fumes? When is enough enough?

_____

_____

EXERCISE 8 (Focus 6)

State the implications of the following rhetorical questions taken from various published texts.

EXAMPLE: Should your children have to struggle with the same difficult and confusing dictionary you had?

IMPLICATION: _They shouldn't have to struggle with the same difficult and confusing dictionary you had._

1. You've fought the good fight. You've reached the top. Now isn't it time you treated yourself to what you really deserve?

_____

_____

2. That high-priced box of sugar-coated cereal may taste good, but two slices of bread and a glass of milk is equal to the entire box in food value. Even with the more expensive whole wheat breads, I can buy two loaves for the cost of one box of cereal. Who needs all that sugar anyway?

_____

_____

3. Stereo A has all the buttons and switches and flashing lights you could ever desire, but is it the gadgets that deliver the sound that you want? Stereo B has none of the gizmos above. Its simple case and elegant finish house superb and durable circuitry. And what's more, it costs less.

_____

_____

4. The generals announced their long-awaited truce with an aerial bombardment (fireworks, their press called it). Freedom of speech meant shutting up anyone who had anything to say. This is liberty? This is peace?

_____

_____

5. With the new Voyager GPS 2000, you can find your way back to any landmark, destination, or campsite, anytime. The hand-held GPS 2000 uses satellite navigation technology to instantly pinpoint where you are, where you've been, and where you're going. It's rugged, waterproof, compact, and surprisingly affordable. Isn't this exactly what you've been waiting for?

_____

_____

EXERCISE 9   (Focus 6)

Write a leading question to express each of the following opinions. More than one form is possible, and some ideas may need to be rephrased, not just transformed into a question. State the positive implication of each in parentheses.

EXAMPLE: Opinion: Tropical rain forests are important for the whole planet.

Possible questions and implications: _Aren't tropical rain forests_

important for the whole planet? (They are.)

Doesn't the whole planet benefit from tropical rain forests? (It does.)

Shouldn't we preserve tropical rain forests? (We should.)

1. All young children need to be vaccinated.

_____

_____

2. The sales of powerful herbs should be regulated.

_____

_____

3. We waste too much money on the administrative side of our health care system.

_____

_____

4. Winter is a great time for a vacation.

_____

_____

5. It's better to be safe than sorry.

_____

_____

UNIT 15

Conditionals: Only If, Unless, Even Though, Even If

EXERCISE 1 (*Focus 1*)

Fill in each blank with the appropriate form of the verb in parentheses.

1. If Martin Luther King, Jr., _____ (be) alive today, what _____ he _____ (say) about the current state of race relations?

2. It is not unusual to hear people talking about things they regret not having done. If I _____ (take) such and such a course or _____ (study) with so and so, I _____ (have) a much more interesting job.

3. If you _____ (look) up at the stars tonight around ten o'clock, in the northwest, you _____ (see) the planet Jupiter near the constellation Draco.

4. Norma is an exceptional gymnast and it's too bad she didn't get to be on the Olympic team. I have no doubt that if she _____ (train) just a little harder, she _____ (be) on the team.

5. If my father _____ (take) a book with him on vacation these days, it usually _____ (be) a thriller.

6. If you _____ (smoke) and _____ (eat) fatty foods, you _____ (run) the risk of having heart problems.

7. I'm glad my children are all grown up. If they _____ (be) teenagers now, I _____ (not allow) them to watch MTV.

8. If you _____ (want) to drive while you are in Europe, you _____ (have to) get an international driver's license before you go.

9. Why didn't you say something? You know that if you _____ (ask), I _____ (help).

10. If I _____ (buy) stocks in Microsoft ten years ago, I _____ (be able) to retire already.

11. Petra's family was very strict about eating. If the children _____ (not eat) all their meat and vegetables, they _____ (not get) any dessert.

12. If I _____ (study) German seriously throughout the year, I _____ (not feel) as lost as I did when I was there last summer.

13. My grandfather told me that if I _____ (graduate) summa cum laude next May, he _____ (buy) me a car.

EXERCISE 2 (Focus 2)

Rewrite the following sentences using *only if* instead of *unless* and making other changes as necessary.

EXAMPLE: This program will not run properly unless you increase your RAM.

This program will run properly only if you increase your RAM.

1. You will not qualify for a scholarship unless you maintain a B average.

   _____

   _____

2. Our team will win tonight unless our three top players get injured.

   _____

   _____

3. You shouldn't take out a loan unless you are sure you can repay it.

   _____

   _____

4. No one was invited to the reception for the president unless they had contributed a lot of money to the campaign.

   _____

   _____

5. We did not get second helpings at dinner unless we asked politely. _____

   _____

   _____

EXERCISE 3 (Focus 2)

Decide whether *if, only if, even if,* or *unless* should be used in each blank.

The Struggle for Equality

A major theme throughout history is the struggle of particular groups against prejudice and segregation. Just thirty years ago, in many parts of the American South, **(1)** _____ you were white you couldn't sit at the front of a bus nor eat at certain restaurants. Furthermore, blacks were barred entry to many universities and colleges in the South **(2)** _____ they had excellent high school grades. **(3)** _____ the school had established quotas for minority students was there any chance of being admitted. In some cases, blacks were admitted **(4)** _____ they had scholarships. The civil rights legislation enacted in the 1950s and 1960s played a significant role in overcoming inequality and discrimination.

Nevertheless, even today, restrictions barring certain people have not been lifted from many private clubs. **(5)** _____ you are black or a woman there are still places—country clubs and club rooms especially—where you will not be likely to gain admittance. So exclusive are some of these clubs that **(6)** _____ you are a white man, you would be granted access **(7)** _____ you are a member and are wearing a suit and tie.

Flight Information

For domestic flights you should be at the airport one hour ahead of time **(8)** _____ you do not have any bags to check in, in which case you can show up thirty minutes before the scheduled departure. Once aboard the aircraft, you should put your carry-on bag in the overhead compartment **(9)** _____ it cannot fit beneath the seat in front of you. Thanks to the efficiency of computer networks, your travel agent can give you your seat assignment and boarding pass in advance but **(10)** _____ you purchase your ticket more than two weeks before departure. Unfortunately, once your ticket has been made out, you cannot change your return flight **(11)** _____ you pay a penalty.

EXERCISE 4 (Focus 3)

Express these statements from an automotive manual more emphatically by beginning each sentence with *only if* or *not unless*. Make any other changes you think are needed.

EXAMPLE: You should use the jack to change a flat tire only if your vehicle is on flat ground.

> Not unless (or Only if) your vehicle is on flat ground should you use the jack to change a flat tire.

1. Your engine will not run smoothly unless you change the oil regularly.

_____

_____

2. The treads of your tires will wear evenly only if you keep the tires properly inflated.

_____

_____

3. You need to add a special anti-freeze solution to your windshield washing fluid only if you live in a climate where temperatures drop below freezing in the winter.

_____

_____

4. When checking transmission fluid, you will obtain an accurate reading on the level gauge only if the temperature of the fluid is between 60° and 80° C.

_____

_____

5. Your vehicle will not be able to run on leaded gasoline unless it was made prior to 1980.

_____

_____

EXERCISE 5 (Focus 3)

Match the conditions and results and write a complete sentence beginning with **Only if** or **Not unless**. Make any other necessary changes. The first one has been done for you as an example.

CONDITION	RESULT
1. You get a good job	**a.** You should buy a complicated and expensive camera
2. I am totally exhausted	**b.** I was allowed to use the family car
3. You are a serious photographer	**c.** You should light up a cigarette in someone's house
4. I exercise every day	**d.** I feel healthy and relaxed
5. The book is overdue	**e.** I can fall asleep in a noisy hotel
6. The danger of frost has passed	**f.** They turn on their heat
7. They are freezing	**g.** I will agree to marry you
8. You ask and receive permission	**h.** You have to pay a fine
9. I washed it and cleaned it	

1. _Only if you get a good job will I agree to marry you._

2. _____

3. _____

4. _____

5. _____

6. _____

7. _____

8. _____

9. _____

EXERCISE 6 (Focus 4)

Complete each of the blanks by forming a negative conditional statement with the cues in parentheses, which give conditions that are contrary to fact. Use *if...not* or *unless* as appropriate. In cases where both are possible, use *unless*. Add any words or phrases you think are needed.

> EXAMPLE: Some months ago, the former administrative assistant warned Terry, who was about to take over her job, that she would have trouble keeping track of the reference books circulating in the department. Terry is pleased that she compiled a data base of all the reference books because
>
> _unless she had done so, she wouldn't know where the books were_
>
> (do so / not know where the books were)

1. Maria is having an easy time revising her essays this semester. She is happy she learned how to use the computer because _____

_____

(not know word-processing / have to spend a lot of time rewriting)

2. This morning I received an urgent letter from an environmental organization looking for my support. It says that _____

_____

(not stop the timber industry / virgin forest be destroyed)

3. When I saw her yesterday, my friend Gertrude broke the bad news of her having been turned down once more after a job interview. Gertrude wondered whether "Honesty is the best policy" was the best maxim in looking for a job. Actually _____

_____

(not be so frank and outspoken / get the job she wanted)

4. Richard is going to France this summer and feels confident and excited. He told me that

_____

_____

(not find someone to practice French with / not feel so confident)

5. My grandparents came from Russia and never really learned to speak English well, and I never learned much Russian. Now that they are gone, I really regret this because _____

_____

_____

(not speak only English / understand more about grandparents)

6. It's not difficult to discover one of Virginia's passions. Go into her apartment and you'll see tapes and CDs all over the place. _____

_____

(not such a great music lover / not have so many tapes and CDs)

7. Most people admit that violent crime is a major problem. Although the gun lobby feels otherwise, many believe that _____

_____

(be harder to get a gun / number of murders decrease)

8. Tony has been feeling sick for the last two weeks. His friends have been urging him to make an appointment to see a doctor. _____

_____

(have health insurance / go to see a doctor by now)

9. The south of the country has been experiencing drought conditions. Farmers are worried because _____

_____

(rain soon / crops be ruined)

EXERCISE 7   **(Focus 5)**
_____

Choose the correct form—*even though* or *even if*—for each blank.

1. _____ he is confined to a wheelchair and is deprived of speech, the British astrophysicist Stephen Hawking has made major contributions to our understanding of the universe.

2. Speak to any successful writer about finding a publisher; he or she will tell you that you've got to keep trying _____ you receive a hundred rejections.

3. Because of his good sense of humor, his wonderful ability to mimic, and his dramatic use of gestures, my friend Sam makes himself understood no matter where he travels _____ he speaks no more than a few words of any foreign language.

4. During the Great Depression of the 1930s, many people, _____ they had college degrees, wound up having to scramble for whatever work they could get. My lawyer grandfather, for example, sold leather belts on streetcorners for a time.

5. I am utterly amazed that she still smokes _____ her uncle, a heavy smoker, recently died of lung cancer.

6. When my great grandmother was growing up, she lived on a farm and everyone in her family had to rise early in the morning _____ it was cold and dark and they were still tired.

7. _____ he had a good lawyer and a plausible alibi, the defendant was found guilty by the jury and sentenced to a prison term.

8. Along with Henry David Thoreau and John Muir, Aldo Leopold is among the most frequently quoted authors in conservation circles today, _____ the public has had limited access to his work.

9. The Victorians found it impossible to dismiss Darwin _____ many were repelled by his ideas that we share a common ancestor with the apes.

10. In a democratic society, people must accept the decision of the majority _____ it runs contrary to their own viewpoint.

EXERCISE 8 (Focus 6)

When made into complete sentences the information in the columns below will be a list of travel tips about staying in London. Make advice statements by combining information in the condition and advice columns. Use an appropriate conjunction: *if, only if, unless, even if,* or *even though*. Make any changes necessary. The condition statement can either begin or end your sentence.

ADVICE	CONDITION
1. don't get on the tube in rush hour	**a.** you feel comfortable driving on the left
2. take the river boat up the Thames to Hampton Court	**b.** you are a foreign visitor
	c. you want a feeling of the countryside
3. don't rent a car	**d.** you're prepared to stand
4. go to visit the crown jewels on a weekend	**e.** you want to know about the history of the city
5. check to see that the flag is flying over Buckingham Palace	**f.** it's not your fault
6. expect to pay 15 percent VAT (value added tax) when you purchase anything except food or books	**g.** you have studied English in North America for several years
	h. your time isn't limited
7. be sure to visit the London Museum at the Barbican	**i.** you want to know when the Queen's in residence
8. be prepared to encounter accents and dialects that will perplex you	**j.** you don't mind waiting in line for at least an hour
9. always say "sorry" when you bump into someone	
10. take a stroll on Hampstead Heath, London's largest park	

1. _____

2. _____

3. _____

4. _____

5. _____

6. _____

7. _____

8. _____

9. _____

10. _____

EXERCISE 9—REVIEW   (*Focuses 1–6*)

Complete the crossword puzzle.

ACROSS

3. *Even though* means "_____ the fact that."
4. Ben likes fishing so much that he goes _____ if it's cold and raining.
5. *Only if* is used at the beginning of a sentence for _____.
8. When describing the past, *if…not* indicates that the condition is _____ to fact.
11. Even _____ he went to many parties, Max never enjoyed himself.
12. _____ unless the forest is moist and relatively warm will there be any mushrooms.

DOWN

1. I don't think I would've understood the physics lecture _____ I had done special research.
2. If I _____ her, I wouldn't be so proud.
6. If you hadn't sat down next to me on the bus, we never _____ have spoken to each other.
7. If you _____ mentioned it, no one would have known.
9. _____ if you go will I go.
10. _____ bother to see that film unless you like being appalled by violence.

Choose the *one* word or phrase that best completes each sentence.

1. _____ the treaty is ratified will the nation receive any agricultural assistance.
   - (A) Unless
   - (B) If
   - (C) Not only
   - (D) Not unless

2. _____, the arguments for the possibility of extraterrestrial intelligence can be summarized as follows.
   - (A) To summarize
   - (B) Shortly
   - (C) Briefly
   - (D) In briefly

3. Your paper is to have been completed by the end of the next week. _____
   - (A) It should have been graded already.
   - (B) Late papers will be lowered one letter grade.
   - (C) Jane would have gotten an A if she had spent more time on it.
   - (D) It wasn't double-spaced.

4. That store is always open twenty-four hours a day _____ it's a national holiday.
   - (A) if
   - (B) even if
   - (C) even
   - (D) despite

5. You said that you had been waiting here for over an hour, but that _____—this place has only been open for 30 minutes.
   - (A) couldn't have happened
   - (B) should have happened
   - (C) might have happened
   - (D) would have happened

6. The army would have surrendered _____ reasonable terms had been offered.
   - (A) unless
   - (B) even though
   - (C) even if
   - (D) if

7. This experiment has been done hundreds of times before. If you had followed the directions carefully, you _____ the proper result.
   - (A) should have gotten
   - (B) might have gotten
   - (C) could have gotten
   - (D) can get

8. _____, apply a finish coat of polyurethane varnish to the wood after sanding lightly.
   - (A) Final
   - (B) The last
   - (C) Lastly
   - (D) In conclusion

9. _____ it was more or less guaranteed to be useful and profitable, the Edison Labs wouldn't have been interested in experimenting with a new idea.

    (A) If   (C) Not unless

    (B) Even if   (D) Unless

10. After hypothesizing, the first thing is to observe and _____ to verify.

    (A) secondly is   (C) nextly is

    (B) the second thing is   (D) then is

11. She _____ have been sleeping very soundly indeed. How else could the burglars have stolen the painting without her being aware of it?

    (A) could   (C) was to

    (B) should   (D) must

12. There are always fireworks in the park on Independence Day _____ it rains.

    (A) even if   (C) not unless

    (B) even though   (D) if

Identify the *one* underlined word or phrase that must be changed for the sentence to be grammatically correct.

13. Robert <u>shouldn't have checked</u> the oil level in his car regularly. Because he <u>didn't,</u> his
               A   **B**

engine <u>overheated</u> yesterday and <u>was seriously damaged</u>.
      C   **D**

14. The bus <u>would</u> not <u>have crashed</u> <u>unless</u> the roads <u>had not been</u> icy.
             A   **B**   **C**   **D**

15. The children <u>were not allowed</u> outside <u>on Saturday</u> afternoon <u>only if</u> they <u>had finished</u>
                   A   **B**   **C**   **D**

their homework.

16. <u>There are</u> a number of <u>method</u> ballistics experts use <u>to determine</u> the force and path <u>of</u>
     A   **B**   **C**   **D**

a bullet.

17. If you're sure that <u>you've tried</u> every key three times and that none of them <u>works</u>, I
                      A   **B**

<u>would say</u> that Peter <u>should have given</u> us the wrong ones.
  C   **D**

18. <u>In overall,</u> <u>as we have seen</u>, Ernest O. Lawrence's contribution to particle physics is
     A   **B**

unquestionable <u>even though</u> he did not live <u>to develop</u> the final stages of many of his
               C   **D**

concepts.

19. In <u>order to</u> separate the isotopes follow <u>these steps</u>. <u>At first</u>, place the emulsion <u>in</u> a
     A   **B**   **C**   **D**
vacuum chamber.

20. If computers <u>had not been invented</u> how <u>could we have come to understand</u> such vastly
                                    A   **B**
complex interrelationships such as those presented by global weather patterns? How

<u>could anyone supposed to have analyzed</u> the immensely complex data concerning flow
                          C
and turbulence and <u>discovered</u> the equations that describe these processes?
                            D

21. <u>Would</u> anyone, <u>even</u> in the brightest of circles, <u>have thought</u> such a solution possible
     A   **B**   **C**
<u>only if</u> a mere five years ago ?
   D

22. I <u>would never have done</u> what Sally <u>did</u>. She went over to pet a wild fox that <u>was sleeping</u>
       A   **B**   **C**
in the woods and it bit her. She <u>should have not done</u> that.
                         D

23. <u>Unless</u> it <u>weren't</u> for the two previous drought years, the reservoirs <u>would</u> now <u>be</u> at
     A   **B**   **C**   **D**
capacity.

24. <u>Must</u> the Indians of Central America <u>have been</u> in contact with Asians in ancient times?
     A   **B**
There is a striking body of evidence based on a comparison of artistic and architectural

forms which <u>suggests</u> that there <u>was</u> probably some kind of interchange.
               C   **D**

UNIT

16 Reducing Adverb Clauses

The following letter from your intrepid Aunt Nelly concerning her latest trek in the Himalayas contains a number of full adverbial clauses. Underline them and then rewrite the letter using the reduced form for each.

Greetings from the roof of the world!

While I am waiting for a helicopter to arrive, I'm taking advantage of the time to write you a quick letter. Let me go back to the beginning. After we spent a couple of days in Kathmandu, we took a bus to a little village where our porters were assembled. It was wonderful to get on the trail. When we started out we were at a low elevation in a semi-tropical landscape, but the trail led ever upward, and in three days, we were among steep cliffs and towering mountains. I've never seen so many waterfalls. After we had trekked for a week, we came to the snow zone. I was glad I had brought a lot of warm clothes. The water in my canteen froze every night! Before we climbed the high pass, we had to stay in one place for a couple of days so we could get used to the altitude. If you don't acclimatize, you can get very sick. Even so, while I was huffing and puffing my way to the top of the pass, I had a headache and wobbly knees. But the pain was worth it. The view was spectacular—jagged peaks everywhere, like a frozen stormy sea.

Unfortunately there was an accident on the way down. While he was scrambling over loose rock, Pete, a member of our party, fell and twisted his ankle. Luckily, the next village wasn't far. But Pete can't continue; his ankle is very swollen and he can't walk. We radioed for help and a helicopter is on the way. I'm sending this letter with poor Pete, so bye for now, and see you in a few weeks.

Nelly

P.S. Oh, I almost forget to tell you. Before I left the U.S., I bought a pair of those hiking boots you recommended. They've been great.

_____
_____
_____
_____
_____
_____
_____
_____
_____
_____
_____
_____
_____
_____
_____
_____
_____
_____
_____
_____
_____

EXERCISE 2   (Focus 1)

Complete the following sentences by adding reduced adverb clauses of time. Use _before, after, while,_ and _when_ to introduce the clauses.

EXAMPLE: _Before choosing a class_____, you should read the course
                    description in the catalog.

1. _____, you should talk to a counselor.

2. _____, you should buy the required
texts.

3. _____, you should take notes.

4. _____, you should raise your hand and
ask a question about it.

5. _____, you should contribute
thoughtfully.

6. _____, you should try to get some
physical exercise.

7. _____, you should get a good night's
sleep.

Rewrite the following folk tale, transforming each full adverbial clause into a reduced form.

Don't Count Your Chickens Before They Hatch

There once lived a woman called Truhana whose family members were beekeepers. Because she wasn't very rich, she had to go to the market every year to sell the family's honey.

As she had a long way to go, she had a lot of time for her thoughts to wander. Along the road she walked, carrying the jar of honey upon her head. Because she was daydreaming, she began calculating the money she would get for her honey. "First," she thought, "Since I will get a good price for the honey, I will buy eggs. The eggs I'll then set under my brown hens, and in no time, there will be plenty of little chicks. Soon they'll become plump chickens, and I'll sell them and buy lambs."

Truhana then began to imagine even grander things. "Because they love lamb so much, everybody will be willing to pay dearly, I'm sure. And since I'll make so much money, I'll soon be richer than my neighbors. That will be so wonderful. I can hardly wait to see the looks on their faces when they see me dressed in finery! And as I'll be rich and respected, I'll marry off my children to the wealthiest people in town!"

Trudging along in the hot sun, she could see her fine sons and daughters-in-law, and how the people would say that it was remarkable how well-off she had become, who was once so poor and low.

Because she was taking so much pleasure in her fantasy, she began to laugh gaily, and preen herself, when suddenly, she struck the jar with her hand and it fell from her head, smashing upon the ground. The honey became a sticky, dirty mess.

Since she saw clearly now the ruin of her dreams, Truhana collapsed on the ground and wept bitterly.

_____

_____

_____

_____

_____

_____

_____

_____

_____

_____
_____
_____
_____
_____
_____
_____
_____
_____
_____
_____
_____
_____
_____

EXERCISE 4   (Focus 2)

The famous Sherlock Holmes and his assistant, Dr. Watson, were staying in an old hotel in the country. During the night, Watson tapped on Holmes's door to tell Holmes he heard strange noises below. Suggest a reason (cause) for each of Holmes's actions by adding a reduced adverbial clause to each sentence below.

EXAMPLE: _Hearing someone at the door_____, Holmes got out of bed.

1. _____, Holmes went softly but quickly down the stairs.

2. _____, Holmes inspected the room thoroughly.

3. _____, Holmes went to the window, which he noticed was open.

4. _____, Holmes went out.

5. _____, Holmes shone his light into the bushes.

6. _____, a young boy trembled.

7. _____, Holmes gently put his hand on the boy's shoulder.

8. _____, Homes asked the boy what he'd been doing in the house.

9. _____, the boy told Holmes the truth.

10. _____, Holmes laughed.

(Focus 3)

Provide a reduced clause for each sentence in the following story. The first one has been done for you.

1. _____Hitting a reef in a storm_____, the ship was destroyed.

2. A man, _____, floated in the ocean for a day.

3. _____, he drifted onto shore.

4. On his hands and knees, _____, he thanked God for sparing his life.

5. _____, he found he was on a small island.

6. He began to explore, _____.

7. _____, he made a meal.

8. Fortunately for him, he found, _____, some useful tools.

9. He made a crude shelter, _____.

10. One day, _____, he wondered who else was on the island.

EXERCISE 6 **(Focus 3)**

Continue the story from Exercise 5. Use reduced clauses in different positions. Share your story with other members of your class.

_____

_____

_____

_____

_____

_____

_____

_____

_____

_____

_____

_____

_____

_____

Match the following main clauses and participial phrases. Try placing the participial phrases in different positions, using commas as necessary.

EXAMPLE: The Panama Canal, completed in 1914, allowed ships to pass between the Atlantic and Pacific Oceans without having to make the long journey around Cape Horn. (3, g)

PARTICIPIAL PHRASES

1. Rising 1,250 feet,
2. Built by Shah Jahan in the seventeenth century as a mausoleum for his wife,
3. Completed in 1914,
4. Extending over 1,500 miles,
5. Hoping to control floods, create new arable land, and supply electricity,
6. Completed by the emperor Titus in 80 A.D.,
7. Derided by many when it was finished in 1889,
8. Installed in 1856,

MAIN CLAUSES

a. the Great Wall of China, which was begun in the 3rd century B.C., was not completed until more than a thousand years later.
b. the Coliseum in Rome was used for gladiatorial contests and wild beast displays.
c. the Eiffel Tower has become a beloved symbol of Paris.
d. the Empire State Building in New York City is one of the highest buildings in the world and a top tourist attraction.
e. the bell in the great clock tower of the Houses of Parliament in London was named "Big Ben" for Sir Benjamin Hall, commissioner of works.
f. the Taj Mahal in Agra, India, is considered by many to be the most beautiful building in the world.
g. the Panama Canal allowed ships to pass between the Atlantic and Pacific Oceans without having to make the long journey around Cape Horn.
h. Egypt, with Soviet assistance, built the huge Aswan High Dam between 1960 and 1970.

1. _____

_____

2. _____

_____

3. _____

_____

4. _____

_____

5. _____

_____

6. _____

_____

7. _____

_____

8. _____

_____

EXERCISE 8   (*Focus 4*)

Complete the crossword puzzle using emotive verbs in the correct forms.

ACROSS

1. The child, _____ by the shadow on the wall, dove beneath the bedcovers.
4. The book was banned because of its _____ content.
6. No one can be _____ without good manners.
7. _____ by the unwanted attention, the young visitors could hardly wait to leave the reception.
9. Her smile and the twinkle in her eye clearly showed that she was _____.
10. _____ as the manuscript was, the scholars found it a fabulous find.
11. _____ and unworthy of its reputation was how all of us found the celebrated film.

DOWN

1. He tore up his paper, _____ by his poor grade.
2. The speaker, though _____ with his audience, continued to smile as he answered their rude questions.
3. The tourists were utterly _____ in the railroad station by the crowds and the noise.
5. _____ by the title, Edward decided to see the film.
8. _____ the picnickers, the black flies buzzed around their heads.

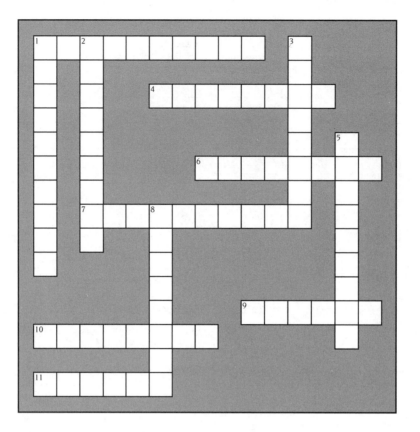

Some of the following sentences are correct and others are incorrect because of dangling participles. Mark "correct" those sentences without errors. Rewrite the sentences that have dangling participles.

EXAMPLE: After working for hours, the garden looked beautiful.

After working for hours, Jane made her garden look beautiful.

1. Sniffing under the hedge, Sam spotted an opossum cleaning the yard.

_____

_____

2. The dolphins, leaping up to catch fish, delighted the spectators at the aquarium.

_____

_____

3. After hiking all day long, the thought of a tent and a sleeping bag was very attractive.

_____

_____

4. The hunter shot the rhinoceros charging down on him.

_____

_____

5. Having planted bulbs in fall, many flowers grew in spring.

_____

_____

6. Racing down the highway because he was already late for work, the road seemed very long to Robert.

_____

_____

7. The icy wind, blowing into the cabin through every crack, made the hikers huddle together for warmth.

_____

_____

8. Frustrated by overly complicated questions, the test was infuriating.

_____

_____

9. Hoisted up to the fifth floor with a heavy rope, the movers brought the piano in through the window.

_____

_____

10. Putting on sunglasses, the glare wasn't so bad, he thought.

_____

_____

UNIT

17 Preposition Clusters

EXERCISE 1 (*Focus 1*)

Complete the following sentences by choosing a verb and a preposition from those listed in the columns below. Use each choice only once.

VERBS		PREPOSITIONS	
approve	decide	about	on
comment	pay	for	to
complain	praise	of	
consent	rely		
count	think		

EXAMPLE: The Olympic team **was praised for**_____ its extraordinary dedication and discipline.

1. You can't _____ the weather being nice every day.

2. I refuse to _____ the repair of a machine under warranty.

3. The teacher _____ the excellent work of the class.

4. The couple _____ getting married quickly and without ceremony.

5. The candidate _____ withdrawing from the race rather than risking defeat.

6. It doesn't make sense to _____ winning the lottery.

7. I advise you to _____ the impact your example will have on your younger brothers and sisters.

8. None of my friends _____ smoking in public places.

9. Do the students always _____ the food in the cafeteria?

10. She _____ doing things herself, without relying on her family for everything.

Complete the crossword puzzle with verbs relating to sight and facial expressions.

ACROSS

1. The child _____ at her little brother after her mother blamed her for making the mess.

4. It's not polite to _____ at people.

5. "Look, that clown is _____ at us! I wonder why?"

7. I had so much work to do last night that I only _____ at the first pages of the report before going to bed.

8. The teacher _____ at the student's paper, which was folded and smudged.

9. The embarrassed guest sheepishly _____ at the hostess after he had spilled his drink.

DOWN

2. "After you've drained the oil, would you mind _____ at the brakes too?"

3. The tourists at the Hollywood studio _____ at the film stars in wonder.

4. The two burglars _____ at each other when they found the door unlocked.

6. The football player _____ at his opponent, who was making insulting remarks.

Write sentences of your own with the subjects and verbs listed below. Use each only once. Add an object of your own choice and a reason or explanation for the association.

EXAMPLE: the managers   united with

The managers united with the workers in declaring a strike.

SUBJECT	VERB + PREPOSITION
1. my parents	**a.** associate with
2. the police	**b.** cooperate with
3. community members	**c.** consult with
4. the administration	**d.** deal with
5. I	**e.** join with
6. the minority political party	**f.** side with
7. my great uncle	**g.** unite with

1. _____

2. _____

3. _____

4. _____

5. _____

6. _____

7. _____

Fill in one of the following verbs + *from* in each blank.

abstain	deviate	emerge	recede	separate
desist	differ	escape	recoil	shrink
detach	dissent	flee	retire	withdraw

1. According to Hinduism, there are four stages of life. The first stage is that of student. A student's chief obligation is to learn, and, as an apprentice, he is under the guidance of a teacher whom he must not **(A)** _____. The second stage, the physical prime of life, is that of the householder with its obligations to family and community. The third stage occurs when the person **(B)** _____ the busy world of work. Any time after the arrival of the first grandchild, the individual may **(C)** _____ the social obligations he has assumed in order to devote himself to philosophical inquiry and self-understanding. The final stage is that of the "sannyasin," the wise man who has come to a clear understanding of life and who is completely **(D)** _____ the strivings of the world. The sannyasin has no fixed residence, no belongings, no goal, no pride, and no expectations. Finally, he is free.

2. Heinrich Harrer was a German mountaineer who was captured by the British while on a climbing expedition in India at the beginning of the Second World War. His first two attempts to **(A)** _____ the prison camp were failures. But on the third attempt he succeeded. **(B)** _____ his British and Indian pursuers, and then later from bandits, he made his way through Tibet to the capital, Lhasa, where he eventually became a tutor of the current Dalai Lama.

3. The southern states **(A)** _____ the policies declared by Abraham Lincoln. As a result they decided to **(B)** _____ the Union.

4. My cousin Ralph always felt he was a square peg in a round hole. With his strange hairstyles, weird clothing, and outrageous opinions, he clearly **(A)** _____ the norm. Though he **(B)** _____ violence, he could never say no to the promises of pleasure, which were typically in the forms of drugs and alcohol. He became an addict and total drop-out and many of his former friends wound up **(C)** _____ him. Fortunately, he found his way to a treatment center and began putting his life in order. When I saw him at a dinner last week, he told me he had **(D)** _____ drugs and alcohol for two years now. I was impressed by how healthy and cheerful he looked and I wished him continued luck.

Fill in the blanks with an appropriate verb + *for*. Try to use a different verb for each sentence.

ask	hope	pray	wish
crave	long	thirst	yearn

EXAMPLE: Anyone who has lived under a repressive political system knows what it's

like ___**to long for**___ freedom.

1. My mother is a very religious person and every day she _____ her family and world peace.

2. "I'm sorry, but this isn't what I ordered. I _____ apple pie, not chocolate cake."

3. There is a school of thought in contemporary psychology that maintains that an addict, on a very basic level, _____ wholeness.

4. My sister Joan, who is a runner presently recovering from an injury, _____ the day when she'll be able to run freely again.

5. It's interesting that when you are on a special diet, you _____ things you shouldn't have, even if you didn't often eat them before.

6. When I travel by airplane, I usually _____ a window seat so I can see the view.

7. Winter can seem very long to people who live in the northern part of the United States. Usually, sometime in February, people begin _____ Spring.

8. In the U.S., it's customary for people to _____ something before blowing out the candles on a birthday cake.

Fill in the blanks with an appropriate adjective + preposition cluster. Try to use a different one for each sentence.

afraid of	homesick for	safe from
eager for	ignorant of	sorry for
enthusiastic about	proficient in	unhappy about

EXAMPLE: A good student is a person who is ___**eager for**___ learning.

1. A xenophobic person is one who is _____ foreigners.

2. A secure person is one who feels _____ harm.

3. A repentant person is one who feels _____ what he or she has done.

4. A naive person is someone who is _____ the ways of the world.

5. A depressed person is one who is deeply _____ the way things actually are.

6. Nostalgic persons are those who are _____ their former homes or the past.

7. A polyglot is one who is _____ several languages.

8. A fan is someone who is very _____ a team, a player, or some activity.

<table>
<tr><td>**EXERCISE 7**</td><td>**(Focus 5)**</td></tr>
</table>

Match the following organizations with their goals or purposes using one of these clusters: *interested in, concerned about, accustomed to, committed to, dedicated to,* or *preoccupied with.*

EXAMPLE: *UNESCO is dedicated to developing education internationally and arranging scientific and cultural exchanges.*

ORGANIZATION	GOAL/PURPOSE
1. World Wildlife Fund	a. preventing and treating birth defects
2. Mothers Against Drunk Driving (MADD)	b. protecting threatened wild places
3. National Trust for Historic Preservation	c. preventing blindness in developing nations
4. CARE	d. preserving historic buildings
5. Sierra Club	e. reducing the number of alcohol-related automobile accidents
6. March Of Dimes	f. protecting the diversity of animal life and setting up protected parklands for wildlife
7. International Eye Foundation	g. providing relief to countries in need

1. _____

_____

2. _____

_____

3. _____

_____

4. _____

_____

5. _____

_____

6. _____

_____

7. _____

EXERCISE 8 (Focus 6)

Complete the following sentences by supplying an appropriate beginning for each by writing *in* (*the*) or *on* (*the*) in the following blanks.

EXAMPLE: ___In the_____ event of rain, the picnic will be postponed to next Friday.

1. _____ advice of my physician, I regret to inform you that I shall have to resign my post.

2. They had to cancel school for the rest of the week _____ account of bad weather.

3. All those _____ favor of the proposal say "Aye."

4. _____ process of investigating the atom and nuclear reactions, scientists discovered subatomic particles.

5. Pull the red switch in the elevator only _____ case of emergency.

6. The Smiths have different ways of winding down after a day's work. He goes out jogging while she's _____ habit of sitting down and watching the news.

7. _____ basis of economic necessity, the city council had to reduce the number of hours the library would stay open on weekends.

8. The teacher had to give William an "incomplete" for the course. There were two major papers he didn't hand in, and his attendance was erratic. _____ top of everything else, he didn't show up for the final examination.

9. The department of maintenance and operations is _____ charge of a multitude of jobs from repairing leaky pipes to running the campus post office.

EXERCISE 9 (Focus 6)

Fill in the following blanks with the expressions below.

at odds with	in the course of	on account of
by means of	in the name of	on the strength of
in return for	in the process of	with the exception of

1. _____ the continuous influx to America, the American people have been a perpetually changing mixture of diverse cultures.

2. _____ history, the character of the American people has been renewed in each generation. It has never really existed in a definitive form.

3. _____ kidnapped Africans, the history of American settlement from the beginning was the record of people in search of promises, or, as some have said, of "castles in the air."

4. _____ the tales, both true and misleading, that they had heard of extraordinary New World gifts for the taking, early settlers came eagerly to this country, their promised land.

5. Every group that has come has found the country occupied by people who arrived earlier. Each great wave of immigrants met resistance and found themselves in some way _____ the ruling establishment.

6. Early traders exchanged iron tools and pots, blankets, firearms, and whiskey with the Indians _____ furs, but tragically, _____ this exchange, the Indians' independence and self-sufficiency eventually gave way.

7. _____ its language, the British left a lasting stamp on America.

8. The early Pilgrims in the Massachusetts Bay Colony began all legal contracts with the phrase, "_____ God, Amen."

EXERCISE 10 (Focus 7)

Complete the following sentences by introducing a topic or identifying a source. Add a noun phrase as necessary. Use each of the clusters below at least once.

According to	Pertaining to	Speaking of
Based on/upon	Relating to	With respect to

EXAMPLE: **Speaking of food** _____, let's go get some lunch.

1. _____, a large number of automobile accidents occur just after sunset.

2. _____, it certainly makes revising papers easier.

3. _____, consumers are gaining confidence in the economy once again.

4. _____, the defendant was clearly on the premises on the night of the crime.

5. _____, there is $250.00 deductible.

6. _____, there has been a curious disappearance of frogs around the world.

7. _____, they accomplished some incredible things.

8. _____, the best diet is the one that gives you the most energy.

9. _____, who do you think will win the NBA championship?

10. _____, a major outbreak of flu is expected this winter.

UNIT

18 Gerunds and Infinitives

Read the following text and underline all gerunds and infinitives. Then identify the function of each.

(1) If you think a failing memory is an inevitable consequence of growing older, think again.

(2) "Over the last 10 years we've learned that even in advancing age, the brain can continue to grow and to adapt," says Dr. Curt Sandman, co-director of the Memory Disorders Clinic at the University of California at Irvine. **(3)** The key to maintaining a good memory, researchers say, is to think of the brain as any other muscle that needs regular "workouts" to keep from getting out of shape.

(4) One of the newest workouts for improving memory is memory-training classes, offered through some colleges and universities. **(5)** After 10 sessions of memory training, participants over age 60 scored from 10 to 50 percent higher on memory tests.

(6) A memory course can help you draw on all the senses, emotions, and rational processes that affect how memory works. **(7)** Sharpening listening skills and expanding visual memory are some of the things people can learn at any age along with techniques on how to mentally file information for easier recall.

(8) Video exercises are often a key component of memory training. **(9)** A typical exercise may begin with the instructor showing a slide of a number of unrelated objects (such as a comb, a spoon, and a pen) and asking participants to remember them. **(10)** Few can, until shown how to, establish a connection between the objects through a phrase, size, material, or function.

(11) Another video technique teaches people to associate names with faces. **(12)** They are asked to exaggerate a prominent feature on screen and to superimpose an image on the face that corresponds to the name—for example, a bird's beak for a man named Bill.

(13) To find a memory-training course, start by calling the psychology department or counseling service of your local university or community college.

(Adapted from "Lessons that can improve your memory" by Eve Glicksman, *Good Housekeeping*, September 1994.)

Complete the crossword puzzle.

ACROSS

1. With our new factory, our intention is to be _____ two hundred machines a month.
2. _____ refused a credit card was a humiliation for Joan.
3. The fighting must come to an end, the leaders agreed. We must find a way _____ _____ this senseless conflict.
7. Even though she didn't get any of them in the end, Claire felt that _____ _____ nominated for three prestigious fellowships was an honor in itself.
10. We were proud indeed to have _____ a personal telephone call from the president herself.

DOWN

1. To be _____ was all the struggling writer wanted.
4. It's always easy _____ _____ the solution in retrospect.
5. We really regret _____ _____ that film. We had bad dreams for a month afterward.
6. To have _____ _____ for no apparent reason was the chief grievance the twenty terminated workers had.
8. _____ on the Internet is easy once you have a computer, a modem, and the right software.
9. We were hoping _____ _____ saved enough money to build a house by this time.

Match the information in the two columns and write a complete sentence with it, making the first part an infinitive or gerund. Add any words you feel are needed to improve the sentence. The first one has been done as an example.

A	B
1. make new friends	**a.** not a sport for those who suffer from vertigo
2. change old habits	**b.** you must make sure you are grounded
3. climb a mountain	**c.** a lot of what firefighting is all about
4. get caught for cheating	**d.** takes lots of willpower
5. save lives	**e.** essential to running a successful household
6. pay the bills on time	**f.** can be the cause of undue stress
7. before doing anything inside a computer	**g.** all my family wanted me to do
8. make a chocolate cake	**h.** a challenge to many children especially when they enter a new school
9. succeed in school	**i.** first mix two cups of flour with sugar and baking powder
10. stay in good shape	**j.** a disgrace in my family
11. try too hard	**k.** you must exercise for at least one hour every day

1. _Making new friends is a great challenge to many children, especially when they enter a new school._

2. _____

3. _____

4. _____

5. _____

6. _____

7. _____

8. _____

_____

9. _____

_____

10. _____

_____

11. _____

_____

EXERCISE 4 (*Focus 4*)

Match the information in the two columns and write complete sentences with it, using infinitives or gerunds in the second part. Add any words you feel are needed to improve the sentence. The first one has been done as an example.

A	B
1. Louis Pasteur's hope	a. speak English fluently
2. Genghis Khan's desire	b. behead some of his wives
3. What Abraham Lincoln is remembered for	c. conquer the world
4. My personal dream	d. help nations develop
5. Goal of the Peace Corps	e. have a hit song
6. One of the things Henry VIII is remembered for	f. work all the time
7. Ambition of every rock group	g. emancipate black people from slavery
8. One reason to become a doctor	h. receive praise
9. What a workaholic enjoys	i. eradicate infectious disease in the world
10. What everyone loves	j. alleviate suffering

1. <u>Louis Pasteur's hope was to eradicate infectious disease in the world.</u>

2. _____

_____

3. _____

_____

4. _____

_____

5. _____

_____

6. _____

_____

7. _____

_____

8. _____

_____

9. _____

_____

10. _____

_____

EXERCISE 5 (Focus 4)

Fill in the blanks below with appropriate infinitives. More than one answer may be possible.

EXAMPLE: The desire __to be healed__ is necessary for anyone recovering from a serious illness.

1. Ask anyone in the healing profession and he or she will tell you that the motivation _____ is a natural part of the human spirit.

2. For people who suffer from hypertension, the suggestion _____ can be enhanced through the use of a gentle voice and soothing background music.

3. In yoga and relaxation classes, the teacher often gives the instruction _____ of tension.

4. Often patients who have been through programs send each other suggestions _____ their exercise and relaxation programs.

5. It is a fact that when people get the encouragement _____ they most often do so.

6. Many doctors make the recommendation to patients _____ a certain time every day for special healing practices.

7. In many hospitals there are plans _____ stress-reduction clinics.

8. It is common today for bored people _____ too much.

Fill in the blanks with the adjective complement of your choice. The first one has been done for you as an example.

The trekking party was anxious **(1)** __to set off__ early in the morning. The way ahead was going to be strenuous but everyone was in excellent shape and high spirits. This was the last day of a 28-day trek among some of the highest mountains in the world. There was one high pass ahead of them that they were likely **(2)** _____ by noon and they were determined **(3)** _____ there. Everyone in the party was tired and eager **(4)** _____ out of the mountains before winter came on. The party made good time. As they neared the top of the pass they were excited **(5)** _____ the fabulous views. Towering peaks, massive glaciers, and steep canyons were everywhere. Reaching the top of the pass, the party was surprised **(6)** _____ so many clouds racing up from the south. In no time, it seemed, the wind grew cold and ferocious. Everyone was shocked **(7)** _____ a storm coming up so quickly. They were reluctant **(8)** _____ so they decided to continue. Roping themselves one to the other, they were careful **(9)** _____ together. However, conditions quickly grew worse. After taking careful compass readings and consulting their maps, they realized they were just above an open plateau. They were hesitant **(10)** _____ the plateau with a major storm about to break. Since they were all afraid **(11)** _____ in the open they took shelter in a cave. They were fortunate **(12)** _____ because just then the storm broke. It was a massive blizzard and the wind howled all night.

The storm abated with the dawn and the party was delighted **(13)** _____. It was difficult going because of all the newly fallen snow, and progress was slow. They made it into the trees by nightfall. They set up camp and made a meal. They were fortunate **(14)** _____ extra provisions with them because now they were two days behind schedule.

Fortunately the next day everything went well and they reached their destination by midafternoon. Everyone was happy **(15)** _____ in civilization again. Some members of the party considered themselves lucky **(16)** _____.

Read the following sentences. Write OK beside the correct sentences and make all necessary corrections to those that are incorrect.

EXAMPLE: Please don't forget ~~picking~~ *to pick* up the children after work.

1. _____ The movie was so good I couldn't stop to watch it.

2. _____ Did I mention my accepting their invitation to dinner?

3. _____ Jonathan can't stand eating in smoky restaurants.

4. _____ The ambassador assured the trade delegation that their country would continue benefiting from our technical assistance.

5. _____ I used to hate to eat meat when I was young, but my parents forced me to.

6. _____ Madam, we regret to inform you that your dog has not been found.

7. _____ The crew failed to repair the hatch in time.

8. _____ Her lawyer advised her dropping the case.

9. _____ Thanks a lot. I really appreciate your mention that to him.

10. _____ After he had shot his cousin by mistake, the hunter vowed never to touch a rifle again.

11. _____ Would you hesitate helping someone in need even if it would put your life at risk?

12. _____ God forbade Adam and Eve to pick any apples from a certain tree.

13. _____ The consultant urged them not to release the report until the latest figures were in.

14. _____ Gauguin hated to live in France and yearned painting on a warm and exotic Pacific island.

15. _____ The senator reminded his secretary to cancel his appointment with the newsman.

16. _____ I don't deny to visit her but I advise you to stop questioning me about it.

17. _____ She appears having trouble finishing her report.

18. _____ Our biochemistry prof said he expected us putting in no less than six lab hours per week

19. _____ I like to imagine him being happy, the way he was that enchanted summer.

20. _____ Another hurricane like the last one will cause this sea wall to collapse.

PART A

As you read the following text, circle all gerund complements and underline all infinitive complements. (Not every sentence will have one.)

PART B

Make a list of the verb + infinitive or gerund combinations that you find.

EXAMPLE: **verb + infinitive**   **verb + gerund**

be unable + to concentrate   begin + tutoring

America's Great Inventor, Thomas Edison

(1) Thomas Alva Edison, born in 1847, was America's most prodigious inventor, with over 1,093 patents to his name. **(2)** He was a mischievous and inquisitive boy who, at the age of six, set the family barn on fire, "just to see what would happen." **(3)** At school he was unable to concentrate and was forced to leave because his teacher found him "addled." **(4)** His mother, a former teacher, began tutoring him at home and soon had him reading Shakespeare, Dickens, and Gibbon.

(5) At age 12, he launched his business career, hawking newspapers and other things on the train that ran between his hometown and Detroit. **(6)** He set up a lab in the baggage compartment that caught fire one day when one of his experiments exploded. **(7)** He learned to operate the telegraph, and during the 1860s, he wandered the country. **(8)** He often neglected his duties to use the lines for experiments—and once blew up a telegraph station while tinkering with a battery. **(9)** He drifted to New York City, and before long, started to invent things. **(10)** When he was 22, he engineered his first successful invention, an improved stock ticker that could keep up with the frenzied speculation of the New York Stock Market. **(11)** Edison earned $40,000 for the invention and with that he began manufacturing telegraphic equipment. **(12)** His next major invention was the diplex method of telegraphy whereby one line could carry up to four messages at the same time. **(13)** Successful and finally established, with a lab of his own and assistants, he devoted the rest of his life to experimenting and inventing.

(14) "Anything that won't sell, I don't want to invent," he said. **(15)** Not a scientist or thinker in the way that Newton and Einstein were, Edison cared little about advancing scientific knowledge. **(16)** Instead, he became absorbed in making marketable products and making them quickly. **(17)** Moving to a new "invention factory" (the first large-scale industrial research laboratory) at Menlo Park, New Jersey, in 1876, he soon began taking out one patent a month. **(18)** Wax wrapping paper, the mimeograph machine, and a commercially viable telephone were some of the wonders that flowed from the Edison Labs.

(19) Edison was testing ways to record telegraph messages when he stumbled onto the principles of his most unique invention, the phonograph. **(20)** Before a few co-workers in 1877, he shouted "Mary had a little lamb" into an apparatus that looked like a small hand-turned lathe with a needle that scratched a groove in the tinfoil. **(21)** He then put the needle back in the starting position and a scratchy, squeaky nursery rhyme came back out of the machine.

(22) In 1878, Edison turned his attention to perfecting a safe and inexpensive electric light to replace oil lamps and gaslights. **(23)** He tried out numerous materials to see if they would carry a current and glow: coconut fibers, lamp wick, fishing line, even hairs from a friend's beard. **(24)** Finally he tried passing a current through a carbonized thread in a vacuum—and it worked. **(25)** No system existed to make and distribute electricity to the consumer, and so Edison went on to design a flurry of new products: screw-in sockets, light switches, insulated wire, meters, fuses, conductors, underground cables, a generator, and even the central power station. **(26)** In so doing, he changed forever the face of the American home and workplace. **(27)** The age of electricity was born.

(28) Oddly enough, in all his long and distinguished career, Edison made only one important scientific discovery, the Edison effect—the ability of electricity to flow from a hot filament in a vacuum lamp to another enclosed wire but not the reverse, but because he saw no use for it, he failed to pursue the matter. **(29)** He attributed his own success to sheer perseverance; in his own words, "Genius is one percent inspiration and ninety-nine percent perspiration."

PART B

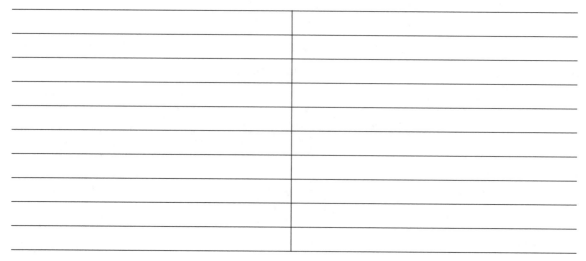

(Focus 4)

Complete the following sentences based on the passage in Exercise 1. Use *to* + verb or verb +-*ing*.

> EXAMPLE: As a young boy, he liked ___*doing*___ things "just to see what would happen."

1. Edison's mother decided _____ him at home.

2. At age 12, Edison began _____ business on a train.

3. Experimenting, he caused a baggage car _____ fire.

4. Undaunted by accidents, he kept on _____ and succeeded in _____ a telegraph station.

5. In New York City, Edison managed _____ a machine that proved invaluable to the stock market.

6. With the invention of his stock ticker, Edison started _____ big money.

7. He hired a crew of technicians _____ for him at Menlo Park.

8. Edison's next major invention was the diplex method of telegraphy, which allowed one line _____ four messages at once.

9. Edison did not care about _____ things that wouldn't sell nor was he concerned with _____ scientific knowledge.

10. In making the first phonograph, Edison learned how _____ sounds.

11. Edison hoped _____ oil lamps and gaslights with an inexpensive light bulb.

12. Edison did not delay _____ many new electrical products.

13. Edison's many inventions and conveniences encouraged the consumer _____ electricity.

EXERCISE 10 **(Focus 5)**

Read the descriptions of the situations. Below each description is a comment on the situation. Fill in the blank with *for* + noun/pronoun or a possessive construction to complete each comment.

> EXAMPLE: Jenny didn't train very hard for the cross-country race. The two best runners on the opposing team came down with the flu. Jenny won the race.
>
> ___*Jenny's*___ winning the race was lucky.

1. Bob was late for an important meeting, so he was driving at more than 20 miles an hour over the speed limit. A hidden police car was monitoring traffic with a radar. Bob was caught and heavily fined.

   _____ having been caught speeding was most unfortunate.

2. Maria went to the races and placed a bet. She won a small amount and then, thinking it was her lucky day, she bet more than a thousand dollars on a horse. The horse came in last.

_____ betting so much money wasn't very wise.

3. Karl drove thirty miles to go swimming in a pool. When he got there he found the pool was closed for cleaning.

Karl was very disappointed at _____ being closed.

4. The Kumars bought a brand new car last week. This week it broke down.

_____ to develop engine problems was outrageous.

5. We spent a lot of time and money trying to help our candidate get elected. He lost the election.

_____ losing the election was a blow to the party.

6. Eve worked very hard during all of her high school years. She applied to a good college and received a full scholarship. Her family was very proud and delighted.

_____ receiving a full scholarship was great reason for _____ to rejoice.

7. A timber company wanted to harvest an old-growth forest. They were opposed by environmentalists and the case went to court. The court decided in favor of the timber company.

_____ getting the okay to cut down an old forest was bad news to environmentalists.

8. Pieter applied for a job with a company he had always wanted to work for and was deeply disappointed when he didn't get it. A few months later the company filed for bankruptcy.

Everyone thought that _____ not getting the job he wanted was really a blessing in disguise.

9. Our local high school was having budget problems. The school board decided to drop all foreign language programs.

We thought that _____ having to drop its language programs was a misguided decision.

A democracy is a form of government by the people either directly or through representatives. The majority of countries in the world today have some form of democratic government. A representative parliament, regular elections, universal suffrage, and basic freedoms and rights are all hallmarks of a democracy.

Write general statements about these ideas, using the prompts below. Include verb + -ing or to + verb in each response.

EXAMPLE: democracies   believe in   (power of the leaders is limited)

Democracies believe in the power of the leaders being limited.

1. democracies   insist on   (holding free elections on a regular basis)

2. democracies   call for   (people vote whenever they want to determine the level of popular confidence in the present government)

3. candidates   argue about   (spend money for projects and programs)

4. voters   hope for   (elected officials do what they promised during their campaigns)

5. people   consent to   (accept the verdict of the majority)

6. people   complain about   (elected officials forget their promises)

7. elected officials   think about   (get re-elected)

Complete the following dialogues, using one of the following phrasal verbs and verb + *ing*.

carry on	go through with	put up with
cut down on	look forward	take up
give up	toput off	

EXAMPLE: Don't you use salt any more on your food?

I've cut down on using salt after reading the latest medical findings.

1. I'm surprised to see you. I thought you were going to visit your parents this week.

_____

_____

2. I can't believe you're quitting your job. What's the problem?

_____

_____

3. What are you going to do in France this summer?

_____

_____

4. I thought your mother stopped that treatment a few months ago.

_____

_____

5. Hey, George, old pal, what's up? Haven't seen you at the pub in ages.

_____

_____

6. What are you doing now that your kids are away at college?

_____

_____

7. You look tired. Didn't you get any sleep last night?

_____

_____

Read the following notes about important modern inventors. Write sentences about each person, using one of the following expressions: *be celebrated for, be famous for, be good at, be proficient in, be renowned for, be skillful in,* or *be successful in.*

EXAMPLE: Benjamin Franklin, American statesman, diplomat, and author, invented the lightning rod, the Franklin stove, and bifocals.

Benjamin Franklin was an American statesman, diplomat, and author who was famous for inventing the lightning rod, the Franklin stove, and bifocals.

1. James Watt, Scottish engineer, invented the steam engine.

_____

_____

2. Robert Fulton, American inventor, improved the steamboat and the submarine.

_____

_____

3. Samuel Colt, American inventor and industrialist, pioneered mass-production techniques and the use of interchangeable parts.

_____

_____

4. Joseph Henry, American physicist and educator, guided others in research leading to famous inventions such as the telegraph and telephone.

_____

_____

5. Enrico Fermi, Italian physicist, built the first nuclear reactor.

_____

_____

6. Count Ferdinand von Zeppelin, a German aeronautical engineer, perfected the hot-air balloon.

_____

_____

7. George Eastman, an American inventor and manufacturer, invented the Kodak camera, the first easy-to-use popular camera.

_____

_____

TOEFL®

Test Preparation Exercises
Units 16–18

Choose the *one* word or phrase that best completes each sentence.

1. Just as he was about to leave the house, Fred thought about the possible showers later in the afternoon and remembered _____ the bedroom windows.
    (A) closing   (C) close
    (B) to close   (D) to having closed

2. _____ taking Thursday off, I suggest we take Friday.
    (A) In place of   (C) In lieu of
    (B) On grounds of   (D) In the event of

3. His advisors convinced the secretary of defense not _____ the announcement until all the details had been worked out.
    (A) to make   (C) to have made
    (B) making   (D) having made

4. The survivors of the crash, _____ close together for warmth, survived a freezing night on the side of the mountain.
    (A) since huddled   (C) after huddled
    (B) because huddling   (D) huddling

5. The street sweeper, _____ in abject poverty, ran after the man he saw drop his wallet.
    (A) though living   (C) after living
    (B) though lived   (D) lived

6. _____ her husband who was abroad making a film, she accepted the award and thanked the committee.
    (A) On account of   (C) On behalf of
    (B) On the strength of   (D) On grounds of

7. The Speaker of the House frowned _____ the disrespectful comments he heard coming from the upstairs gallery.
    (A) about   (C) against
    (B) from   (D) at

8. If we really want to get the grant, I suppose we'll have to put up with _____ numerous forms.
        (A) to fill out   (C) having filled out
        (B) filling out   (D) to have filled out

9. _____, the medicine finally began to have some effect on the inflammation.
        (A) Taking a tablet four   (C) After I took a tablet four times
            times a day   a day
        (B) After taking a tablet   (D) My taking a tablet four times
            four times a day   a day

10. The vice president of sales and marketing convinced _____ the revolutionary new software even before all the bugs had been worked out.
        (A) the CEO to announce   (C) to announce
        (B) the CEO announcing   (D) announcing

11. During the War of the Spanish Succession from 1701 to 1713, the English and the Dutch switched allegiance from Charles of Austria in order to _____ Philip of Spain so as to prevent the union of France and Spain.
        (A) deviate from   (C) side with
        (B) sneer at   (D) cooperate for

Identify the *one* underlined word or phrase that must be changed for the sentence to be grammatically correct.

12. When the board of trustees suggested <u>to raise</u> the tuition for the second time within
                                  A
three years, several members of the administration <u>questioned how</u> the institution <u>was</u>
                                          B
<u>going to</u> continue <u>to attract</u> students from middle income families.
  C   **D**

13. The language of the inscription was <u>bewildered</u> <u>even to</u> the team of <u>dedicated</u> specialists
                               A   **B**   **C**
<u>who had studied</u> historical dialects in the region for decades.
    D

14. <u>Because</u> <u>having signed</u> the contract, the company knew <u>it would be</u> responsible
  A   **B**   **C**
<u>in the event of</u> damages.
    D

15. <u>Irritating</u> by <u>the lack of</u> attention, the <u>frustrated</u> customer began <u>to shout</u> his demand for
  A   **B**   **C**   **D**
a refund.

16. The two companies finally <u>called off</u> their negotiations <u>with regard to</u> a possible merger
                        A   **B**
<u>because</u> one of the companies was reluctant <u>to have accepted</u> a new chairman.
  C   **D**

17. While the British controlled India, many families were in the process of summering in the
      A   B

cool hills where they built bungalows, laid out gardens, and escaped from the
                                        C   D

overwhelming heat in the lower elevations.

18. The inventor Nikola Tesla quit working for Thomas Edison because he believed him
                                 A   B

to have been cheated out of a promised bonus for having improved Edison dynamos.
      C   D

19. As they looked around the exam hall, the teachers couldn't help noticing that the
      A   B

students were anxious for themselves to begin the test.
                        C   D

20. Despite using torture on top of solitary confinement, the prison authorities did not
                        A   B

succeed in getting the political prisoner to cooperate with them and to dissent against
      B   C   D

the party he had helped to found.

21. Although he was fond of acting and singing rather than playing music himself, the
      A   B

emperor Nero is famous at having fiddled while Rome burned.
              C   D

22. The pet importing company reluctantly agreed to the government inspecting of all of the
                                                    A

crates and cages in the warehouse that had come in from South America and Africa, even
                                    B   C

the ones that had already received initial clearance.
          D

23. It was the proposal to wearing school uniforms that made the principal popular with
            A   B   C   D

some of the parents.

24. According a recent study of bird behavior done in the course of research by Lance
      A   B

Workman, a Welsh animal psychologist from the University of Glamorgan, robins, like

humans, develop regional accents, and will even become vexed in the event of hearing
                                        C   D

songs by members of the same species who hail from different places.

Perfective Infinitives

EXERCISE 1 (*Focus 1*)

Complete each blank with a perfective infinitive, using the verb in parentheses.

EXAMPLE: That is a fascinating topic for you *to have explored* (explore).

1. The motive appears _____ (be) one of honor rather than passion.

2. The fanatics believed themselves _____ (act) correctly despite the grief they caused.

3. _____ (waste) so many taxpayer dollars is a scandal.

4. Gretchen considers the president _____ (made) the wrong decision in his choice of ambassador to Gabon.

5. **(A)** Alan is glad _____ (join) the Peace Corps after having finished college. **(B)** His parents expected him _____ (go) to graduate school right away, but Alan was an idealist who wanted to see the world. On assignment to Tonga, he worked for two years helping to construct and improve houses. One of the things he learned to do particularly well was to make doors. **(C)** He claims _____ (make) at least three hundred of them.

6. **(A)** _____ (dare) to dive from the cliff was something my childhood neighbor, Joe, would always regret. He and I had been following a group of older boys to one of their "hangouts" on a ledge over a shallow pond. We wanted to join their club. **(B)** To become a member you had _____ (do) something risky. They told us to dive off and Joe did so without hesitation but he twisted his back when he hit the water. The injury confined him to a wheelchair for the rest of his life. **(C)** I have always considered myself lucky _____ (stay) put and not obeyed.

7. **(A) Peter:** "It was really nice of the Hendersons _____ (invite) us over.

   (B) Jane: _____ (prepare) such a spread was amazing. The hors d'oeuvres, the pasta, the breads, the salads, the pastries! What a feast!

   (C) Peter: Everything was great. Still, _____ (eat) a bit less would have been better for me.

8. **(A)** I'm not so sure I would have liked _____ (see) Pandora's face when she opened the box. In the myth, Zeus warned her not to open the box, but curiosity got the better of her. **(B)** _____ (resist) would have been impossible for someone so inquisitive. She peeped inside, and out streamed all the evils that plague the world—sickness, age, every vice, and death. **(C)** It was good of Zeus _____ (put in) one last thing, however, and that was hope.

EXERCISE 2 *(Focus 1)*

Complete the sentences with your own words using a perfective infinitive for each.

1. I expect _____

   _____ by this time next year.

2. I believe that this is a worthy project _____

   _____ .

3. To _____

   _____ is one experience I will never forget.

4. It was worth the effort _____

   _____ .

5. John D. Rockefeller had enough money _____

   _____ .

6. I would love _____

   _____ .

7. My parents were very pleased _____

   _____ .

8. To _____

   _____ would have been preferable.

9. It was quite dangerous for _____

   _____ .

EXERCISE 3 *(Focus 2)*

Fill in each blank with a perfective infinitive using the verb in parentheses. Then check the box of the type of past meaning expressed: past relative to the present, to the past, or to the future.

1. Two years ago, Cynthia believed finishing her dissertation _____ (be) a foregone conclusion. She had already done all the class and field work necessary. She was bright, energetic, had excellent organizational skills, and enjoyed writing.

   ❑ relative to the present ❑ relative to the past ❑ relative to the future

2. She was surprised when she became pregnant. The next nine months, though, turned out to be a rich time, one she was always very glad _____ (experience).

   ❑ relative to the present ❑ relative to the past ❑ relative to the future

3. But she had less inclination to spend long hours in the library or in front of a computer screen. Although she had intended _____ (finish) more than half the writing by the time of her daughter's birth, she found herself unable to stick to her original plan.

❑ relative to the present   ❑ relative to the past   ❑ relative to the future

4. Her husband, Byron, was supportive throughout. He was there at the birth of their daughter, Reina, and has always considered it _____ (be) one of the most moving moments he's known.

❑ relative to the present   ❑ relative to the past   ❑ relative to the future

5. In the first months after Reina's birth, Cynthia was too busy with her baby or simply too tired _____ (write) much, although she did manage a chapter. She figured that nothing else could have been done _____ (change) her output.

❑ relative to the present   ❑ relative to the past   ❑ relative to the future

6. Reina is nearly one and things have gotten easier. Everyone is especially thankful for Reina _____ (begin) sleeping through the night. Now everyone gets a good night's sleep.

❑ relative to the present   ❑ relative to the past   ❑ relative to the future

7. When Byron received a promotion recently, he and Cynthia arranged to hire a nanny. With someone to help, Cynthia now expects _____ (make) a lot of progress on her dissertation by the end of the year.

❑ relative to the present   ❑ relative to the past   ❑ relative to the future

EXERCISE 4   (Focus 2)

Restate the infinitives in the following quotations as perfective infinitives. Which do you prefer, the original or the perfective version?

EXAMPLE: "To doubt one's own first principles is the mark of a civilized man." (Oliver Wendell Holmes, Supreme Court Justice)

To have doubted one's own first principles is the mark of a civilized man.

1. "To see what is right and not to do it is cowardice." (Confucius, Chinese philosopher)

_____

_____

2. "To die for an idea is to place a pretty high price upon conjecture." (Anatole France, French author)

_____

_____

3. "There are two tragedies in life. One is not to get your heart's desire. The other is to get it." (George Bernard Shaw, British dramatist)

_____

_____

4. "To interpret is to impoverish." (Susan Sontag, American author)

_____

_____

5. "The easiest person to deceive is one's self." (Edward George Bulwer-Lytton, British writer)

_____

_____

EXERCISE 5 (Focus 3)

Rewrite each of the following clauses (*when* clauses, *that* clauses, or clauses with *that* deleted) as a perfective infinitive clause. Make any word changes that are necessary.

EXAMPLE: Mudita believes that she was misdirected by a sign that had probably been turned.

Mudita believes herself to have been misdirected by a sign that
had probably been turned.

1. Many people consider that America was discovered by Vikings.

_____

_____

2. I'm glad I wasn't living in Paris during the Reign of Terror.

_____

_____

3. The newspaper reported that the high government official had been selling secrets for many years.

_____

_____

4. Imagine my surprise when I opened the vault and found that all the jewels had been stolen.

_____

_____

5. Some people claim that the Nazca Lines in Peru were made by extraterrestrials.

_____

_____

6. Twenty-five years ago the number of sea otters was considered low enough that they were accorded endangered status.

_____

_____

7. They promised that they would do all the work by Friday.

_____

_____

8. Their teacher expects that they will check all their papers for spelling errors.

_____

_____

9. She was thrilled when she was chosen to represent the class at the conference in Washington.

_____

_____

10. The guerrillas claimed that they were educating the people when instead they were terrorizing them.

_____

_____

EXERCISE 6   (Focus 4)

Rewrite each sentence so it contains a negative perfective infinitive clause. Use the pattern for formal written English.

EXAMPLE: The boys never let me into their club but I was always glad I hadn't jumped.

The boys never let me into their club but I was always glad not to have jumped.

1. It would have been dishonorable if we had not tried to do something.

_____

_____

2. Roberto claimed that he had never heard of the assignment.

_____

_____

3. Before he saw the ghost, Scrooge was proud that he had never given away a penny.

_____

_____

4. Although when the police stopped him there was an open whiskey bottle on the seat behind him and a very distinct smell on his breath, the driver of the car claimed that he had not had a drop all night.

_____

_____

5. Many leaders subsequently admitted that they had been wrong when they had not investigated the export of weaponry to belligerent nations.

_____

_____

EXERCISE 7 (Focus 5)

Use the cues below to make sentences expressing a past wish that did not materialize or an unpleasant event that was avoided. Use the standard English pattern of _would like_, _would love_, _would prefer_, or _would hate_ followed by a perfective infinitive. Make any changes that are necessary, including any needed verb tense changes.

EXAMPLE: do all my papers on a word processor

I would prefer to have done all my papers on a word processor.

1. have more time to use the swimming pool

_____

_____

2. be discovered napping in class

_____

_____

3. be given a take-home exam

_____

_____

4. spend longer with my classmates in the cafeteria

_____

_____

5. come down with the flu during the lesson on perfective infinitives

_____

_____

6. be able to use a Macintosh computer

_____

_____

7. know how to add graphics to my reports

_____

_____

8. be served coffee or tea in class

_____

_____

9. do even more grammar exercises on my own

_____

_____

10. come to class by mistake when it was a holiday

_____

_____

EXERCISE 8   (Focus 6)

Write sentences with perfective infinitive clauses using the cues. Use a variety of structures and add descriptive words or phrases to expand the sentences.

EXAMPLE: Be wonderful…spend a month in Hawaii.

It must have been wonderful to have spent a month relaxing in

Hawaii.

OR

It was absolutely wonderful to have spent an entire month in Hawaii

surfing, kayaking, and hiking.

1. Be a miracle…escape alive.

_____

_____

2. Be sweet…send a cake and a gift.

_____

_____

3. Be shocked…read about the latest scandal.

_____

_____

4. Be generous…spend time doing volunteer work.

_____

_____

5. Be unacceptable…come to the event in old clothes.

_____

_____

6. Be thrilling…hang-gliding.

_____

_____

7. Be tedious…work on an assembly line.

_____

_____

8. Get together…be marvelous. (Start with _for_ + noun)

_____

_____

9. Be irritating…get caught in a traffic jam.

_____

_____

EXERCISE 9 (_Focus 7_)

Make up sentences with _appear_ or _seem_, followed by a perfective infinitive, for each of the following situations.

1. You are stopped on the road by a police officer. He asks to see your driver's license. You look for your wallet and can't find it. Give an appropriate response.

_____

_____

2. You go with a couple of friends to a rock concert. The lead singer is slurring his words, crashing into the guitarists, and falling down on the stage. You make a comment to your friends.

_____

_____

3. You are in a restaurant with your family. The waiter brought you your menus ten minutes ago and has not returned to take your order. You make a comment.

_____

_____

4. You are a teacher. A student hands you a paper done on the computer but the print is very faint and barely legible. Make a comment to her.

_____

_____

5. You are in a hotel. You have asked for a nonsmoking room. You go to your room and find there are ashtrays in several places and cigarette burns in the bathroom. You return to the reception desk. Make an appropriate response.

_____

_____

EXERCISE 10 **(Focus 8)**

You are a student at a job interview and are being asked the questions below. Respond using the same main verb but use a phrase indicating time and add a perfective infinitive and any information you feel is appropriate.

1. What courses do you expect to have finished by June?

_____

_____

2. What, other than academic coursework, do you plan to have done before you graduate?

_____

_____

3. What other companies do you intend to have visited before you make a job commitment?

_____

_____

4. Was there ever a time when you were supposed to have done something but found yourself unable to for whatever reason?

_____

_____

5. What do you hope to have accomplished within the next five years?

_____

_____

Use the phrases below to create sentences about past possibilities, using perfective infinitives.

EXAMPLE: weather…hot enough

The recent weather was hot enough to have made me want to move to a place with a more moderate climate.

1. drank enough coffee

   _____

   _____

2. movie…scary enough

   _____

   _____

3. slide show…boring enough

   _____

   _____

4. storm…snowy enough

   _____

   _____

5. be tired enough

   _____

   _____

6. salesman…convincing enough

   _____

   _____

The following sentences express disbelief about an event or explain why something didn't happen. Combine the ideas in each pair of sentences into one sentence, using a perfective infinitive clause.

EXAMPLE: The plants in the garden couldn't have survived. It was too cold last night.

It was too cold last night for the plants in the garden to have

survived.

1. Derek couldn't have gone to see such a frivolous show. He's too serious.

2. Dr. Mayer wouldn't return his students' essays without comments and corrections. He's far too dedicated a teacher.

3. They couldn't have slipped the guns through. The border's too well guarded.

4. That lawyer couldn't have lost the case. His arguments were too convincing.

5. We couldn't have believed his excuses. They were somehow too contrived.

UNIT 20

Adjective Complements in Subject and Predicate Position

EXERCISE 1 (*Focus 1*)

In the following short texts, complete the adjective complements.

EXAMPLE: An abandoned and abused Scottish terrier named Bobby kept vigil for fourteen years at the grave of a man who, just before he died, had given the animal a simple meal of scraps. That Bobby _could have been so dedicated_ was remarkable and touching.

1. In 1975, a shipwreck victim off the coast of the Philippines spent two days on the back of a giant sea turtle who, during that time, swam on the surface of the water and did not even dive to feed itself. Turtles typically spend most of their time underwater. For a turtle _____ is unbelievable.

2. In 1950, in Hermitage, Tennessee, a very old woman named Aunt Tess suffered a bad fall at home and would have died but for her canary, who flew to the neighbor's home and beat her wings frantically on the window until she got the neighbor's attention. The canary then dropped dead of exhaustion. A bird's _____ _____ is amazing.

3. A captive elephant known as Bertha lived for years in her trainer's room and didn't smash any of the furniture, even the cabinet where she knew her favorite foods were kept. That is astonishing.

4. Chicken in poultry factories routinely have their beaks cut so they will not be able to inflict harm on each other in their crowded conditions. That _____ _____ is disturbing when you think about it.

5. A German shepherd missed his companion, who had moved from Brindisi to Milan, Italy, and left him behind. The dog set out on a journey of 745 miles and found his old master. For the German shepherd _____ _____ is truly extraordinary.

6. Insects are great masters of disguise. Bugs can resemble thorns; butterflies, with wings closed, can resemble dead leaves; moths can look like patches of lichen; and there is a caterpillar in Costa Rica that has a pattern at its rear end that makes it look like a tiny viper. Insects' _____ is remarkable.

EXERCISE 2 (Focus 1)

Imagine that you have returned to various previous stages of your life. What would make you *happy, eager, anxious,* or *ready*? Write your answers in the first person and use one of the adjectives listed above.

EXAMPLE: baby

I would be eager for my parents to play with me.

OR

I would be happy to splash in the bath.

| 1. baby | 3. 5-year-old | 5. young teenager |
| 2. toddler | 4. 10-year-old | 6. late teenager |

1. _____
2. _____
3. _____
4. _____
5. _____
6. _____

EXERCISE 3 (Focus 2)

Fill in the following blanks with a variety of appropriate linking verbs and adjectives from the following lists. More than one answer may be correct.

LINKING VERBS		ADJECTIVES	
appear	apparent	foolish	regrettable
be	certain	helpful	sad
look	compulsory	impossible	unfortunate
remain	difficult	insensitive	unlikely
seem	disturbing	likely	wonderful
	fascinating	odd	

EXAMPLE: George falls asleep in nearly every class. For him to get a high grade *would be unlikely*.

1. _____ for people to throw away everything they don't want into the trash. They could recycle and help prevent the landfills from overflowing.

2. _____ that people are working harder than ever and don't seem to have much free time. Fifty years ago everyone predicted that people at the end of the twentieth century would have lots of leisure time. That those prophecies didn't come true _____.

3. Pamela's mother is very ill. Her having to drop out of school to look after her mother _____.

4. _____ that the Oxus River has changed its course several times in recorded history. The river's drying up today _____.

5. Samantha is going to spend next year in Argentina and Chile. Her having studied Spanish this year _____.

6. _____ for every adult citizen to vote in Australia.

7. Harry won a national photo contest. For Harry to get such a prestigious award _____.

8. _____ that wearing a seat belt cuts down on the possibility of serious injury in the event of an automobile crash. That anyone would deliberately not wear a seat belt _____.

9. _____ that the world population will double within thirty years. Feeding so many _____.

10. Professor Schwartz didn't inform us that there would be a quiz today. That many of us didn't bother to study last night _____.

EXERCISE 4 (Focus 2)

State your feelings about the following facts found in the *Guinness Book of World Records* (McFarlan et al., New York: Bantam Books, 1989) using a *that* clause in subject position.

EXAMPLE: The most expensive sport shoes obtainable are the mink-lined golf shoes with 18-carat gold embellishments and ruby-tipped gold spikes by Stylo Matchmakers International Ltd. of Northampton, England, that retail for $17,000 per pair.

That someone would spend so much money on a pair of shoes is absolutely unbelievable.

1. Emperor Bokassa of the Central African Empire (now Republic) commissioned pearl-studded shoes from the House of Berluti in Paris for his coronation in December 1977 at a cost of $85,000.

_____

_____

2. The largest collection of valid credit cards is 1,199, all different, owned by Walter Cavanagh of Santa Clara, California (known as "Mr. Plastic Fantastic"). He keeps them in the world's largest wallet, 250 feet long, weighing 35 pounds, and totaling more than $1.4 million in credit.

_____

_____

3. An unnamed Italian industrialist was reported to have lost $1,920,000 in five hours at roulette in Monte Carlo, Monaco, on March 6, 1974.

_____

_____

4. If meanness is measurable as a ratio between expendable assets and expenditure, then Henrietta (Hetty) Howland Green (1835–1916), who kept a balance of over $31,400,000 in one bank alone, was the all-time world champion. She was so stingy that her son had to have his leg amputated because of the delay in finding a *free* medical clinic. She herself lived off cold oatmeal because she was too thrifty to heat it. Her estate proved to be worth $95 million.

_____

_____

5. The highest death toll in modern times from an earthquake has been in the Tanshan earthquake (magnitude 8.2) in eastern China on July 27, 1976. A first figure published on January 4, 1977, revealed 655,237 killed, but that figure was later adjusted to 750,000. On November 22, 1979, the New China News Agency unaccountably reduced the death toll to 242,000. As late as January 1982, the site of the city was still a prohibited area.

_____

_____

EXERCISE 5   (*Focus 2*)

Read the following extracts from "The Daily Diary of Environmental Happenings" for the months of February and March 1993 (from Buzzworm magazine). Then comment on the facts using a *that* clause and the adjective provided.

EXAMPLE: frightening

That our nuclear power stations are so unprotected is frightening.

February 7: Middletown, PA—An intruder crashed his car through a gate and spent four hours hiding inside the Three Mile Island nuclear power plant before he was arrested, authorities said. "Nuclear plants are supposed to be able to protect against terrorists armed with high-accuracy weapons who have insider help," said Robert Pollard, a nuclear safety engineer. "This guy drives into the plant and they can't find him?"

February 12: Boston, MA—A prominent AIDS researcher told the annual meeting of the American Association for the Advancement of Science that as many as 1 billion people may be infected with AIDS worldwide.

March 19: Amsterdam—A Japanese-owned tanker carrying toxic chemicals exploded in the North Sea, killing at least one crew member. Flames as high as 160 feet shot from the ship, a Dutch Navy official said. Authorities said there were no immediate reports of toxic chemical leaks.

March 20: Washington, D.C.—A U.S. attack submarine and a Russian missile-carrying sub collided under the surface of the Arctic Ocean. Neither submarine sustained major damage, authorities said.

March 20: Baghdad—A UN chemical weapons specialist said Iraq has destroyed about 70 tons of nerve gas and about 400 tons of mustard gas, as ordered by the United Nations.

March 24: Los Angeles—The Clinton Administration has designated a small bird, the California gnatcatcher, a threatened species under the Endangered Species Act. Coastal sage scrub ecosystems will be set aside from development to provide habitat for the bird.

1. frightening

_____

_____

2. fortunate

_____

_____

3. unfortunate

_____

_____

4. encouraging

_____

_____

5. shocking

_____

_____

6. good

_____

_____

What would be unexpected or unusual for the following people to do? Write a sentence that expresses your idea. Begin with "For..."

EXAMPLE: a world-class athlete

For a world-class athlete to eat lots of junk food would be unusual.

1. carpenters

_____

_____

2. scuba divers

_____

_____

3. critics

_____

_____

4. vegetarians

_____

_____

5. Buddhist monks

_____

_____

6. ballerinas

_____

_____

7. computer programmers

_____

_____

In the sentences below, decide whether the adjective complements refer to factual information or potential events. Mark the appropriate boxes.

1. Henry is spending most of the day cleaning up his room. Henry's cleaning up his room is pleasing to his parents.

   ❑ factual   ❑ potential

2. Several timber companies are ready to begin cutting in formerly protected parts of the national forests. For old growth forest to be cut is tragic.

   ❑ factual   ❑ potential

3. Many tourists don't bother to learn the languages of the countries they visit. For tourists to communicate well with the people of other countries is rare.

   ❑ factual   ❑ potential

4. Cats are by nature uninhibited predators. That they often play with their prey is shocking to some people but hardly surprising.

   ❑ factual   ❑ potential

5. Ruth doesn't spend a lot of time studying. That she got three As last semester is a miracle.

   ❑ factual   ❑ potential

6. Old aunt Betty doesn't often get visitors. For you to pay her a visit would be very kind.

   ❑ factual   ❑ potential

7. Styrofoam containers, which are commonly used in fast food restaurants, are a major source of litter. It is heartening that some fast food chains have stopped using Styrofoam packaging.

   ❑ factual   ❑ potential

8. The rhinoceros is now an endangered species. It is a pity that rhinoceroses are hunted for their horns.

   ❑ factual   ❑ potential

9. Some managers of nuclear power plants criticize government regulation for being excessive. They would like their strict safety standards to be relaxed. For nuclear power plants to have lax safety standards would lead to a greater incidence of cancer.

   ❑ factual   ❑ potential

10. Monarch butterflies migrate from South and Central America throughout the United States, even to the northern states. That butterflies migrate such vast distances is amazing.

    ❑ factual   ❑ potential

UNIT

21 Noun Complements Taking *That* Clauses

EXERCISE 1 *(Focus 1)*

Complete the crossword puzzle.

ACROSS

1. The city council rejected the _____ to construct a bypass.
2. The proposal _____ restrict the sales of handguns is unacceptable to the gun lobby.
3. The tendency _____ plutonium to become rapidly unstable is well known.
4. Many teachers wonder how they can inspire the necessary _____ for students to achieve real excellence.
9. Scientists believe the _____ that Mars appears red is because the rocks on the surface of the planet contain iron and also because a curtain of fine dust hangs in the atmosphere as a permanent haze.

DOWN

1. We asked the director's _____ to have a party in the cafeteria on Friday after work.
2. Several religions share the belief _____ a redeemer will appear at the end of a time of turbulence to bring in a new age.
5. In 1915, Alfred Wegener proposed the _____ that continents might have moved or drifted.
6. Everyone at Bell Labs applauded the _____ that another one of their researchers had won a Nobel Prize.
7. The _____ that sodium chloride makes up about 85 percent of all minerals in seawater accounts for the saltiness of the sea.
8. You should be aware of the boss's tendency _____ no when he hears a proposal for the first time.

Summarize the information from the text below by completing the statements that follow it.

(1) Without water there is no life, and it is mountains that are responsible for capturing, storing, and delivering water to the lowlands. (2) Historically, the first cultures developed along rivers, which were ultimately fed by the water that came from mountains. (3) The cultures that have thrived for millennia along the Nile, for example, have depended on water that originally fell as rain in mountains as far away as Ethiopia and Burundi. (4) Mediterranean civilizations developed where the Apennine, Atlas, Pindus, Taurus, and other ranges collected sufficient moisture.

(5) Destruction of mountain habitat can produce disastrous results for communities and whole regions as is apparent today in Madagascar, Haiti, and the Philippines, where timber-cutting and grazing have denuded the highlands. (6) Rain on barren hills gathers force with great speed and can generate floods. (7) In addition, valuable topsoil quickly erodes and washes out to sea, and silt may clog irrigation systems and foul drinking water. (8) Without vegetation in higher elevations to help retain precious moisture in the ground, water supplies may cease to exist in dry seasons.

(9) In the mountain ranges of the developing world it is, oddly enough, ambitious aid projects from the World Bank and other agencies that are threatening watersheds. (10) Development schemes involving heavy equipment and the creation of roads for logging and mining can deeply scar the land and precipitate erosion. (11) Dams can drown villages. (12) The toll in terms of disruption to the indigenous people can be severe as villagers are forced from their homelands and are often obliged to seek their livelihoods on unproductive slopes higher up or, abandoning the mountain region completely, in the teeming slums of polluted cities.

EXAMPLE: The fact that ____mountains capture, store, and deliver much of our

____water____ has made them crucial to cultures and civilizations.

1. It is a fact that _____ can cause flooding below.

2. It is a sad thought that _____ to make way for a dam or other development project.

3. The reason that _____ is because there is no longer any vegetation higher up to help retain moisture in the ground.

4. The ironic revelation that _____ is rather shocking.

Which sentence in each of the following pairs contains a noun complement? Circle your choice.

EXAMPLE: **a.** The request that we contribute more money was turned down.

b. The request that you submitted is under consideration.

1. **a.** She denied the allegation that her family could have had a few skeletons in the closet.

   b. She denied the allegation that the newspaper reported.

2. **a.** The advice that I invest my inheritance is a good one.

   b. The advice that the judge gave the new attorney was thoughtful.

3. **a.** Does anyone here believe the notion that the earth is flat?

   b. Does anyone here believe the notion that Russell brought up?

4. **a.** The time that he referred to was undefined.

   b. I will always remember the time that he came to visit.

5. **a.** The chairman made a statement that I couldn't hear.

   b. The chairman made a statement that future meetings would be held on Monday.

The following paragraphs describe amazing facts about famous people. Make observations about each set of facts using a *that* clause following *the fact/idea/news*, etc.

EXAMPLE: The great Austrian composer Mozart died at the early age of 35. He left behind over 600 works, including 50 symphonies, more than 20 operas, nearly 30 piano concertos, 27 string quartets, 40 violin sonatas, and many other instrumental pieces, some of which date from the time he was only four years old.

The fact that Mozart could have achieved so much in such a short lifetime is a clear indication of his genius.

1. On Christmas Day in 1871, Thomas Edison took time out from his busy inventing schedule to marry 16-year old-Mary Stilwell. He didn't take that much time, though. An hour after the service he was back at work in the lab solving another problem.

_____

_____

2. The polio virus was responsible for crippling hundreds of thousands of people in the first half of the twentieth century. The epidemics, usually during warm weather, turned summer into a time of terror. Fear of contagion caused entire communities to be quarantined and thousands of people to cancel vacations. In 1955, the American scientist Jonas Salk created an effective polio vaccine, and a massive public vaccination program began.

_____

_____

3. After the invention of the telephone, Alexander Graham Bell was acclaimed everywhere. He gave numerous speeches and interviews and joined a multitude of organizations, enterprises, and scientific groups. Yet he was always nervous in public roles and would often hide away to avoid social engagements. He would sometimes lock himself in a bathroom or even hide in an attic until someone found him.

_____

_____

4. Franz Joseph Haydn, often referred to as "the father of the symphony," wrote his famous farewell symphony as a gentle hint to his employer, a member of the aristocratic Hungarian Esterhazy family, that he and the orchestra needed a rest. As the music drew to a close, one musician after another set down his instrument and walked away until there were only two violins left.

_____

_____

5. It was a widely held belief among nineteenth-century intellectuals that the mind was controlled by reason. Sigmund Freud, the father of psychoanalysis, began his career as a student of hypnotism. His work with mentally traumatized patients and his investigation of dreams led him to the realization that the reasoning faculty had far less control over people's minds than was previously believed.

_____

_____

The following text about toxic wastes contains too many *the fact that* clauses. Underline instances of *the fact* in the text. Then cross out those that do not seem necessary or are incorrect. The first one is done for you.

(1) One irony of life in the 1990s is <u>the fact</u> that the healthy, robust athlete may actually be at greater health risk than the inactive person. (2) Individuals at all levels of serious exercise often overlook the fact that they may be taking greater risks than they ever imagined due to an unhealthy environment. (3) At least three circumstances are impacting the health of all of us, but because the athlete spends more time in these degraded conditions than the nonathlete, the exposure is greater and so is the risk. (4) The first area of concern is the effect of stratospheric ozone depletion, which allows more intense ultraviolet radiation to penetrate the atmosphere. (5) Each year in the United States, statistics show the fact that approximately 500,000 new cases of skin cancer are diagnosed, and about 70 percent are believed to be the result of exposure of the skin to ultraviolet rays. (6) Most of us can avoid going outside for any length of time in the spring and summer months between 10:00 A.M. and 3:00 P.M., when the sun's rays are the strongest, but this is not the case for professional athletes. (7) In addition to skin cancer, it is now known the fact that cataracts can develop and the immune system can be weakened. (8) The fitness enthusiast is especially affected by air pollution, the second area of concern, because the quantity of air inhaled during exercise and the depth of inhalation into the lungs are significantly greater. (9) The American Lung Association states the fact that running in a typically polluted urban area for 30 minutes is equivalent to smoking a pack of cigarettes a day. (10) A third area of environmental impact on athletes is that of pesticides and toxic chemicals used on athletic turf, from baseball fields to golf courses. (11) Luscious green turf disguises the fact that as much as nine pounds per acre of insecticides, herbicides, and fungicides—all of which can interfere with the human nervous system—lie upon and beneath the attractive surface. (12) Instead of stopping us from playing and working out, this information should give us the determination and incentive to stop the problems. (13) Given the state of our environmental knowledge, we must accept the fact that we must now protect ourselves with creams, sunglasses, hats, and by changing our outdoor exercise schedules, but ultimately, and even more importantly, we must get to the root of the problems and try to effect the necessary changes.

Read the paragraph on the Martinez familly. Comment on the circumstances of the Martinez family using the words below and *the fact/idea/news*, etc., *that* clauses.

Consider the situation of the Martinez family. Carlos and Teresa have four children, Jorge (18 years old), Gloria (16), Guadalupe (13), and Julio (9). The parents have worked hard to provide a nice home and a good education for all of the children. The children have all done well in their school work, particularly Jorge, the apple of his parents' eyes and an honor student who has just received two scholarship offers for college. Jorge himself can hardly wait to leave the tiny home where he has grown up. The brothers share one small room, as do the sisters. Julio chatters a lot and leaves toys and clothes everywhere. The girls are very different from each other. Gloria likes boys with fast cars and Guadalupe likes to read, go to church, and talk to her friends on the phone. The children have frequent arguments.

EXAMPLE: Carlos and Teresa (proud of)

Carlos and Teresa are proud of the fact that
all of their children have succeeded in school.

1. Carlos and Teresa (accustomed to)

_____

_____

2. Jorge (excited about)

_____

_____

3. Jorge (put up with)

_____

_____

4. Gloria (jealous of)

_____

_____

5. Julio (thrilled about)

_____

_____

6. Guadalupe (concerned about)

_____

_____

7. Gloria (annoyed with)

_____

_____

EXERCISE 7　　(*Focus 5*)

Suppose you saw people performing the following strange actions. What would you remind them of in order to help clear up their confusion? Write a sentence about what you would say.

EXAMPLE:　walking on a golf course with bare feet.

I would remind them of the fact that golf courses have high concentrations of toxic chemicals that could be dangerous to their skin.

1. forgetting to say "thanks" when someone helps them or does them a favor

_____

_____

2. lighting up a cigarette in a designated nonsmoking area

_____

_____

3. adding radiator coolant to the windshield fluid reservoir

_____

_____

4. using an infinitive after "enjoy"

_____

_____

5. neglecting to say "excuse me" when they bump into someone

_____

_____

6. going outside in thin clothing when the temperature is below 0° C

_____

_____

7. driving 50 mph on a residential street

_____

_____

The following sentences review the structures learned in this unit. Correct those that contain errors. Write OK next to those that are correct.

EXAMPLE 1: The fact that she contributed so much to charity was laudable.   OK

EXAMPLE 2: She wouldn't accept the notion which some kinds of cholesterol were beneficial to the body.

Correction: _She wouldn't accept the notion that some kinds of cholesterol were beneficial to the body._

1. The possibilities that arose from the new discovery were dazzling.

_____

_____

2. What explains that in some cases the immune system turns against itself?

_____

_____

3. The idea that Martians landed in his backyard was foolish.

_____

_____

4. The news that the drought was over made some people careless in the way they used water.

_____

_____

5. She was conscious of that they were both drifting apart.

_____

_____

6. That disorder must be factored into equations and projections is commonplace in physics.

_____

_____

7. He is always boasting about that he has done two triathlons this year.

_____

_____

8. The notion that we are in full control of our minds is arguable.

_____

_____

9. There are some people who will never accept the notion which we are all born innocent.

_____

_____

10. That he could have gotten away with lying in court is a sad comment on the justice system.

_____

_____

11. The committee supported that the institution had a lot to gain by extending health benefits to part-time employees.

_____

_____

12. The studies which we undertook led to greater understanding.

_____

_____

Choose the one word or phrase that best completes each sentence.

1. It is fantastic _____ the lottery.
   - (A) anyone's to win
   - (B) anyone to win
   - (C) for anyone to win
   - (D) for anyone winning

2. They sent us a letter saying they would have liked _____ to our party last week but were unable due to unforeseen illness.
   - (A) to come
   - (B) coming
   - (C) having come
   - (D) to have come

3. _____ we are indeed living in the best of times may or may not be true.
   - (A) The fact
   - (B) The fact which
   - (C) That
   - (D) It is a fact

4. It is sad _____ of endangered species is a lucrative business.
   - (A) to smuggle
   - (B) about smuggling
   - (C) for the smuggling
   - (D) that the smuggling

5. We had to change our plans because last weekend, with the temperature below 0° F, it was simply too cold for us _____ camping.
   - (A) that we went
   - (B) that we had gone
   - (C) to have gone
   - (D) for going

6. It is a fact _____ ten major tongues, led by Mandarin Chinese, English, Hindi, and Spanish, are spoken by more than 50 percent of the world's population.
   - (A) which
   - (B) that
   - (C) for
   - (D) of

7. _____ on my lawn seems quite remote.
   - (A) That an extraterrestrial landing
   - (B) For an extraterrestrial landing
   - (C) An extraterrestrial to land
   - (D) An extraterrestrial's landing

8. After the accident, he had to face up to _____ full recovery was going to take a long time.
   - (A) the fact that
   - (B) a fact that
   - (C) the fact of the matter
   - (D) that

9. The proposal _____ all high school students to wear uniforms was cheered by some people and scorned by others.
        (A) that   (C) which
        (B) for   (D) about

10. For the poor _____ more taxes than the rich is unjust.
        (A) to have paid   (C) to pay
        (B) having paid   (D) that pay

Identify the *one* underlined word or phrase that must be changed for the sentence to be grammatically correct.

11. He considers <u>himself</u> <u>being</u> lucky <u>to have been</u> the only one in his family <u>not to have</u>
            A   **B**   **C**   **D**
<u>caught</u> the flu this winter.

12. The news <u>which</u> a new oil-indicating mineral called moganite <u>can be found</u> in almost all
          A   **B**
fine-grained quartz specimens <u>may help</u> geologists pinpoint sites <u>holding</u> petroleum
                           C   **D**
deposits.

13. <u>When</u> so many bridges <u>could have collapsed</u> this year is <u>not only</u> terrible but pathetic
      A   **B**   **C**
<u>in light of</u> our industrial strength.
    D

14. When the ambassador's family <u>returned to</u> this country after several years <u>living</u> abroad,
                        A   **B**
I told them that it <u>must have been</u> exciting <u>to be meeting</u> so many interesting people.
            C   **D**

15. The jury <u>was instructed</u> to overlook <u>that</u> the accused had participated in several
        A   **B**
inflammatory rallies and <u>that</u> he was on record as once having advocated the use of force
               C
in the event of a government's attempt <u>to coerce</u> its people.
                          D

16. In a recent discovery <u>made by</u> researchers at Vienna University with an electron
                  A
microscope, the ancient Egyptians <u>appear</u> <u>using</u> silk almost one thousand years earlier
                             B   **C**
than <u>once thought</u>.
    D

17. The suggestion <u>which</u> his aunt, the Archduchess Isabella, <u>intended to employ</u> the painter
   　　　　　　　　A　　　　　　　　　　　　　　　　　　　　　　　　**B**

Rubens on diplomatic missions initially filled King Phillip IV of Spain with doubt, a

feeling <u>that</u> he soon altered <u>after meeting the man</u>.
   　　　C　　　　　　　　　**D**

18. <u>It is</u> interesting <u>about</u> the emperors of ancient Rome were in the habit of <u>making</u> deities
   A　　　　　　　**B**　　　　　　　　　　　　　　　　　　　　　　　**C**

out of personal favorites <u>who had died</u>.
   　　　　　　　　　　　D

19. The old prospector <u>claimed</u> <u>to discover</u> the mine <u>before</u> the mining company <u>got</u> its
   　　　　　　　A　　　　**B**　　　　　**C**　　　　　　　　　　**D**

permit.

20. <u>For</u> everyone is profoundly <u>frightened</u> during times of war <u>is understandable</u> given
   A　　　　　　　　　　　**B**　　　　　　　　　　　　　**C**

<u>the fact that</u> there is almost never a way out.
   D

UNIT

22 Subjunctive Verbs in *That* Clauses

Write a sentence that addresses the indicated situation using a verb of advice or urging + a subjunctive verb. Use the verbs and objects in parentheses and add any other information you feel is relevant.

EXAMPLE: A wife to her husband about their son's expulsion from school (insist/talk to principal)

She insists that he talk to the principal right away.

1. John to Bill about Bill's not being able to see the writing on the blackboard (recommend/see eye doctor)

_____

_____

2. A group of citizens to the police chief about the rising crime in their neighborhood (demand/assign police to their neighborhood)

_____

_____

3. Parents to their teenage daughter about when to get home after her date (insist/get home by midnight)

_____

_____

4. A company memo to all personnel about wearing formal attire while on business trips (stipulate/wear formal attire while on business trips)

_____

_____

5. Betty to her friend in a restaurant about the house special (suggest/try)

_____

_____

6. The town planner to the town council about a traffic problem (propose/ban traffic from the town center)

_____

_____

7. A math teacher to a student about some wrong answers (advise/check figures)

_____

_____

8. A librarian to us about not being so loud (request/lower our voices)

_____

_____

9. The president of the union to the workers about not losing hope (insist /not lose hope)

_____

_____

10. A mother to the judge about her son going to prison (beg/not send her son to prison)

_____

_____

EXERCISE 2   (Focus 2)

Imagine that you are having a conversation with your aunt, Doris, a very concerned citizen who is always phoning people and writing letters to magazines, newspapers, politicians, school principals, the police, and so on. Write Doris's replies to your questions, using the prompts provided and a subjunctive complement.

EXAMPLE: What did the police chief say when you advised him to arrest all teenagers loitering in playgrounds? (ignore/advice)

He ignored my advice that he arrest all teenagers loitering in playgrounds.

1. What did the school principal do when you told him that he should ban pupils from chewing gum while walking to and from school? (laugh at/suggestion)

_____

_____

2. What did the mayor say when you insisted on shops being closed on Sunday? (smile at/demand)

_____

_____

3. What did the editor say about your idea of not printing any story concerning sex or violence? (disregard/request)

_____

_____

4. What did your niece do when you told her she should forbid her children from watching cartoons on television? (not listen to/advice)

_____

_____

5. What did the president do in response to your letter about shutting down all weapons factories in the country? (ignore/plea)

_____

_____

EXERCISE 3   *(Focus 2)*
_____

Imagine that your friend George has recently moved into a new house. Everything is fine except that the neighbors next door have a dog that annoys him very much. They leave it chained up on the deck and it barks all the time. George has already spoken to the neighbors once about this problem, but they insist that their dog never barks. George has asked his friends what to do. Which friends' advice was useful and which wasn't? Write a sentence that expresses your opinion of each friend's suggestion. Try to use as many advice or urging nouns as you can.

EXAMPLE: Fred/call the SPCA (Society for the Prevention of Cruelty to Animals) and report the situation

Fred's advice that he call the SPCA and report the situation was
sensible.

FRIEND	ADVICE
Fred	call the SPCA and report the situation
Kurt	poison the dog
Sally	talk to the dog's owners again
Lisa	make friends with the dog
Rod	release the dog from the chain
Scot	buy earplugs
Kate	get other neighbors to sign a petition

1. _____

2. _____

3. _____

4. _____

5. _____

6. _____

EXERCISE 4 (*Focus 3*)

PART A

The information below is made up from a doctor's notes. Fill in the following statements with *that* clauses containing subjunctive verbs.

EXAMPLE: It is advisable that Ramona T. get an X ray.

PATIENT	COMPLAINTS/ SYMPTOMS	HABITS	RECOMMENDED COURSE OF ACTION
Peter S. / 43	bad cough; difficulty breathing; halitosis	smokes heavily	take cough suppressant; stop smoking
Ramona T. / 52	painful swollen fingers	eats lot of sweets	get X ray; take Advil
Greg A. / 29	pain in knees	jogs 10 miles per day	apply cold pack
Louise M. / 25	nausea, fatigue	perfectionist (newly married)	pregnancy test
Matthew L. / 62	severe chest pains; facial discoloration; gasping	eats fatty foods	immediate hospitalization
Ronnie P. / 38	insomnia	drinks lots of coffee; watches late night TV	take tranquilizer
Samantha C / 11	itchiness/rash on legs	N/A	apply cortisone cream
Corrine D. / 31	fever alternating with chills/red watery eyes	reads one novel a week	flu medication; rest
James H. / 45	headaches/ spaciness/shaky hands/ yellow eyes	drinks heavily	cut down on drinking/ take vitamin supplements
Eleanor K. / 27	depression/ skin lesions	unknown	blood test

1. _____ is vital. (Matthew L.)

2. It is essential _____. (Peter S.)

3. _____ is necessary. (Louise M.)

4. It is important _____. Greg A.)

5. It is desirable _____. (Ronnie P.)

PART B

Create five sentences of your own with information from the chart on page 222.

1. _____

2. _____

3. _____

4. _____

5. _____

EXERCISE 5—REVIEW (*Focuses 1, 2, and 3*)

Complete the crossword puzzle on page 224.

ACROSS

1. The committee's proposal that the town _____ a new bridge over the river was rejected.
3. If someone suffers a deep cut, it is _____ that he or she receive medical attention without delay.
6. In military academies, it is _____ that students wear uniforms to class.
7. The contract _____ that the work be finished by the last day of the year.
9. Irma _____ that we go to a Thai restaurant.
10. The _____ that three hundred workers be let go was received with hostility.

DOWN

2. It is _____ but not required that assignments be done on a word processor.
4. The rebels demanded _____ they have a seat at the negotiating table.
5. Her advice that Peter _____ French I again next semester was hardly surprising.
7. I strongly recommended that Gordon _____ get a promotion and a raise.
8. The teacher demanded that the students _____ on time.

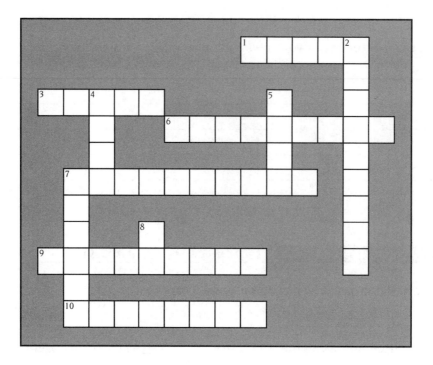

UNIT

23 Emphatic Structures: Emphatic Do, No Versus Not

EXERCISE 1 *(Focus 1)*

Read the following extract from a travel guide and underline examples of emphatic *do* **and** *no* **structures.**

There is no doubt that Africa does have some of the most striking features in the world. The largest desert is there, one of the most extensive rainforests, and the sights of great civilizations such as ancient Egypt. Many travelers have said that there is no sight more beautiful than snow-capped Mount Kilimanjaro rising sheer from the East African plateau. In addition to beauty and vast cultural diversity, Africa offers the largest game reserves in the world. Considering the pressures of population expansion, this is no small accomplishment.

It makes no sense, however, to underplay the dangers or risks in traveling to remote parts of the continent. You do need to keep an eye on the newspapers and your wits together. You do need to keep your eyes and ears open and your mouth in check. Do that and you will have the adventure of a lifetime. This is no package tour, no lazy man's holiday.

All things considered, there is no other continent comparable to Africa. Do make the effort to travel there and experience it for yourself.

(Adapted from Geoff Crowther, *Africa on a Shoestring*: Berkeley; Lonely Planet Publications, 1989.)

Reply to each of the following by making positive emphatic statements. Circle the emphatic form used. Make any other changes that are necessary.

EXAMPLE:　Peter said he isn't going to the party tonight.

Peter is (going) to the party.

1. They didn't like the meal.

2. You won't fix the lawnmower today.

3. They haven't made a movie of *Sense and Sensibility*.

4. You don't have any patience. (add extra emphasis)

5. They aren't going to swim around Manhattan. (add extra emphasis)

6. You didn't notice my new tie.

7. The Senate won't allow old-growth forests to be cut down.

8. Judy hasn't learned how to use the Internet yet.

9. You don't understand what I said. (add extra emphasis)

10. You haven't seen a king cobra in the wild. (add extra emphasis)

Read the following short dialogues and underline all the places where you think it is possible to use emphatic *do*. Rewrite those sentences with an appropriate form of the *do* verb.

EXAMPLE:　**Zara:** It's so nice of you to invite us over.

　　　　　Yoko: Welcome to our home. <u>Sit down.</u>

Do sit down

1. **Mike:** Did you remember to pick up some milk?

   Meg: Yes, I remembered.

   _____

2. **Joey:** I didn't take the money on the table.

   Nita: Oh, then who took the money?

   _____

3. **Ole:** Have you heard that Robert managed to pass the chemistry exam?

   Tuan: I'm glad he passed. Now he won't have any trouble graduating.

   _____

4. **Paula:** It seems that everyone in Darren's family has a major problem.

   Rod: Yes, he has a dysfunctional family.

   _____

5. **Fatima:** Your brother's on vacation, isn't he? Have you received a card from him?

   Aziz: No, he never sends cards.

   _____

6. **Dieter:** How did you like the new Indian restaurant?

   Hilda: Not bad. Even though I don't usually like spicy food, I found the flavors intriguing.

   _____

7. **Esta:** Can I take a walk in your garden?

   Sarala: Of course. It's a bit wet after the rain. Watch out for the puddles.

   _____

8. **Yena:** We just got a huge fine from the tax office. They said we didn't pay our last installment.

   Taylor: That's ridiculous. I paid it. I've even got a receipt.

   _____

9. **Nick:** I like watching golf on TV.

   Jill: You must be kidding!

   Nick: No, I really enjoy the suspense and the skill that you see.

   _____

10. **Carla:** Did you hear that the Bonington expedition made it to the top of Nanga Parbat safely?

    Al: That's great news. When I heard there were storms, I doubted they would make it.

   _____

Read the following story. Then rewrite the story, replacing the underlined phrases with phrases using *no*. The first one has been done for you as an example.

Cinderella—A Fractured Fairy Tale

Poor Cinderella was in a bad position. She had to work all day for her stepmother and ugly stepsisters <u>without a break</u>. She <u>didn't have time</u> to take care of herself, and she <u>didn't have any comforts</u>. She <u>didn't have a warm room, or a soft bed</u> to sleep in.

She could have run away from her mean stepmother and stepsisters, but then she would really have been in trouble because she would have been <u>without food, a home</u>, <u>money</u>, or a <u>job</u>. It seemed as though she <u>didn't have any way out</u>.

On the night of the royal ball, Cinderella was left by herself <u>without friends</u>. She <u>didn't have a dress or a ride</u> to the ball.

Suddenly her fairy godmother appeared and told her not to worry because she could give her dress.

Cinderella said, "No, thank you."

"What?" said the fairy godmother. "If you don't go to the ball, you won't meet your handsome prince and get married; you <u>won't have a husband</u>."

"If it's OK with you, Fairy Godmother," said Cinderella, "I <u>don't want a husband</u>. I'd rather have a good education so I can get a better job."

The fairy godmother agreed with Cinderella and gave her the money to go to school instead of a dress.

Cinderella <u>isn't a princess</u> now; she's a lawyer fighting child abuse.

Poor Cinderella was in a bad position. She had to work all day for her stepmother
and ugly stepsisters with no break.

_____

_____

_____

_____

_____

_____

_____

_____

_____

_____

_____

_____

EXERCISE 5   (*Focus 4*)

You are at the start of your vacation and you are very disappointed with your hotel because it's missing several things that you were promised by your travel agent. Below is a list of the agent's promises. Complain to the hotel manager using emphatic *no* forms.

You will have a beautiful view from your room.

You will have hot water in your room.

You will have clean towels.

You will have air-conditioning.

There will be a lovely swimming pool with clean water.

The restaurant will serve you anything you like.

You will have a private beach.

There will be lots of people to help you.

There will be a taxi available to take you around.

There will be a grocery store within easy walking distance where you will be able to buy provisions.

There will be lots of things for your children to do.

_____

_____

_____

_____

_____

_____

_____

_____

_____

_____

_____

_____

_____

Fronting Structures for Emphasis and Focus

<hr />

EXERCISE 1 (*Focus 1*)

Decide whether the sentences below have fronted structures for emphasis and whether there is subject/verb inversion. Underline the fronted structure if the sentence has one. Circle the subject/verb inversion if the sentence has one.

EXAMPLE: <u>Never in my whole life</u> (have I been) so amused.

❑ No fronted structure ☑ Fronted structure ☑ Subject/verb inversion

1. With great excitement, Judy tore open the letter.

❑ No fronted structure ❑ Fronted structure ❑ Subject/verb inversion

2. Seldom do we eat out nowadays.

❑ No fronted structure ❑ Fronted structure ❑ Subject/verb inversion

3. Because we wanted to have a good view of the stage, we decided to buy the more expensive tickets.

❑ No fronted structure ❑ Fronted structure ❑ Subject/verb inversion

4. The taxes have become so high that many people are considering leaving the area.

❑ No fronted structure ❑ Fronted structure ❑ Subject/verb inversion

5. Rarely did my parents allow us to watch television.

❑ No fronted structure ❑ Fronted structure ❑ Subject/verb inversion

6. In order to cut down on cholesterol, we've changed our diet.

❑ No fronted structure ❑ Fronted structure ❑ Subject/verb inversion

7. Mark not only got his long hair cut but he shaved off his beard too.

❑ No fronted structure ❑ Fronted structure ❑ Subject/verb inversion

8. Nowhere in the town could I find a telephone that was working.

❑ No fronted structure ❑ Fronted structure ❑ Subject/verb inversion

9. I will never make that mistake again.

❑ No fronted structure   ❑ Fronted structure   ❑ Subject/verb inversion

10. Rain or shine, Lois rides her bike to work.

❑ No fronted structure   ❑ Fronted structure   ❑ Subject/verb inversion

---

EXERCISE 2   (*Focus 2*)

Use the cues in parentheses to add a phrase or clause to each sentence. To emphasize the description you added, move it to the front of the sentence. If you wish, you can add other descriptive words or phrases.

EXAMPLE: The creatures chased the mayor. (direction)

Down the long corridors of the city hall, the creatures chased the terrified mayor.

1. The creatures began moving.

a. (time)

_____

b. (manner)

_____

2. The detective spoke with the victim's girlfriend.

a. (purpose)

_____

b. (position)

_____

3. The group approached the great chest.

a. (time)

_____

b. (reason)

_____

4. The scientists saw a city with large pyramids.

a. (position)

_____

b. (manner)

_____

5. Clara phones her mother.

a. (reason)

_____

b. (frequency)

_____

EXERCISE 3   _(Focus 2)_

    Use an appropriate word or phrase from the list below to complete the blanks with fronted structures.

No sooner   Not for anything

Around me   Never

Almost never   Little did I realize

So weak   In the center of the village

Little did we suspect   Fluttering through the air

Not quite as bad as everyone feared

    (1) _____ that morning that I would wind up in a hospital room at night. My wife and I were home again after traveling in Asia for one year. It was a beautiful October day, crisp and clear, and the colors of the leaves were brilliant. We drove to one of our favorite villages. **(2)** _____ were hundreds of colorful leaves. We parked the car and got out with our cameras. **(3)** _____ was a white wooden church. The scent of apples, crushed leaves, and harvested fields was in the air.

    (4) _____ would I have wanted to be anywhere else at that moment. All of a sudden I felt very dizzy. I made my way to the car and curled up in the back seat. I shivered as my wife drove, but by the time we reached home I was hot and sweating. **(5)** _____ had I been ill before, so I was completely bewildered by the waves of cold then heat that were passing over me. **(6)** _____ was I that I could barely climb up the stairs to the bedroom. I collapsed into bed, and after that I remember only strange snatches of feverish dreams until I came to in the hospital. **(7)** _____ were the concerned faces of my wife and the hospital staff. They were glad to see me conscious again. I had been put in a private room because the doctors were worried I might have a contagious disease, caught in the course of my travels. During the night, the cold spells abated, but the fever remained, and I had to sleep with the window wide open and only one sheet. **(8)** _____ was the diagnosis the next day. I had a particularly virulent case of pneumonia. I was treated well and began to recover quickly, but twice daily for the next five days a nurse came to help me clear my lungs. **(9)** _____ have I been pounded so hard on the back.

My wife visited every day and brought with her books and good things to eat. **(10)** _____ that the roles would quickly be reversed. **(11)** _____ did I get home than she came down with the same disease.

EXERCISE 4 (Focus 3)

Make complete sentences by matching items in column A with those in column B.

A	B
1. Never in my life	a. could we take a vacation all together
2. More amazing than ever	b. have nations resolved major disputes without resorting to arms
3. In the parking lot	c. have I laughed so much
4. Rarely in my family	d. is the "I Have a Dream" speech of Martin Luther King
5. More of a health problem than obesity	e. was a famous movie star calling to me
6. Beckoning from the limousine	f. was a chest full of secrets buried in the basement
7. Hidden away, unsuspected,	g. is a beautiful tree that's just come into flower
8. At the top of the Empire State Building	h. was the sight of the little child in tears that I gave her ten dollars
9. Seldom during this century	i. stood a group of awed tourists
10. More inspiring to me than anything	j. is the latest Spielberg film
11. So sad	k. is stress

1. _____
2. _____
3. _____
4. _____
5. _____
6. _____

7. _____

8. _____

9. _____

10. _____

11. _____

EXERCISE 5 (Focus 4)

Add the negative fronted structure in parentheses to the following sentences for emphasis. Make any other changes that are necessary.

EXAMPLE: I will not eat kidneys. (not for any amount of money)

Not for any amount of money will I eat kidneys.

1. That restaurant does not permit smoking. (under no conditions)

_____

_____

2. He has never said he was sorry. (not once)

_____

_____

3. I wouldn't take that drug. (not for anything)

_____

_____

4. She hadn't ever felt so insulted. (never)

_____

_____

5. The theater will not allow children to see that movie. (under no circumstances)

_____

_____

6. I did not realize the complexity of the health care dilemma. (not until recently)

_____

_____

7. This does not alter my opinion. (in no way)

_____

_____

8. They cannot leave the children unattended at home. (in no case)

_____

_____

9. I haven't felt this way. (not since I left home)

_____

_____

10. I have not seen such fascinating architecture as in India. (nowhere)

_____

_____

EXERCISE 6   (*Focus 5*)

Complete the crossword puzzle.

ACROSS

3. _____ was the movie boring but it was also tasteless.
4. I haven't gone swimming this year. _____ have any of my friends.
6. I have never smoked. _____ do I think I ever will.
8. I never expected Stan to get rich. Nor did _____ else.

DOWN

1. Peter won't be here tomorrow. Neither _____ Sandra.
2. No _____ had I fallen asleep than my alarm went off.
5. I didn't understand the author's point. No one else did _____.
6. All the students did well. _____ one person failed.
7. I couldn't get my car up the icy hill. Neither _____ any of the other drivers.

Check what you think is the main reason for fronting each of the underlined structures. Do you think it is primarily for (1) emphasis of the fronted structure, (2) contrast of the structure, or (3) focus on a delayed subject that contains new or unexpected information?

1. <u>On Monday</u>, I'm usually a little reluctant to get out of bed in the morning and begin another week of work. By Friday, the week's tasks nearly at an end, I usually spring right up when I hear the alarm ring.

   ❑ emphasis   ❑ contrast of the structure   ❑ focus on the delayed subject

2. Three quarters of what I get in the mail is either plain junk or charities asking for money. <u>Imagine, then, my surprise yesterday on tearing open a letter to find ten crisp hundred dollar bills inside.</u>

   ❑ emphasis   ❑ contrast of the structure   ❑ focus on the delayed subject

3. <u>When I drive</u>, rarely do I exceed the speed limit. I've never received a speeding ticket and I've never had an accident either.

   ❑ emphasis   ❑ contrast of the structure   ❑ focus on the delayed subject

4. <u>Had you called someone</u> you would have known the class was going to meet at a restaurant instead of at school. Why didn't you phone?

   ❑ emphasis   ❑ contrast of the structure   ❑ focus on the delayed subject

5. Dr. Carter slowly pushed open the door that led into the ancient Egyptian burial chamber. There, <u>spread all along the walls</u>, were heaps of gold and other precious objects.

   ❑ emphasis   ❑ contrast of the structure   ❑ focus on the delayed subject

6. <u>In the front of the building</u> is an opulent marble facade facing a busy street. In the back, the trash bins line a narrow brick alley with fire escapes.

   ❑ emphasis   ❑ contrast of the structure   ❑ focus on the delayed subject

7. <u>Not since before her illness</u> did Alice remember how happy the sight of the sea had made her. After months of pain and struggle, she stood on the beach, with tears of joy running down her cheeks.

   ❑ emphasis   ❑ contrast of the structure   ❑ focus on the delayed subject

8. Rumors spread through the restaurant like wildfire. Everyone was soon more interested in the door than in what was on their plates. <u>And then, finally, unbelievably, framed in the entryway</u> was the President of the United States and the First Lady.

   ❑ emphasis   ❑ contrast of the structure   ❑ focus on the delayed subject

9. <u>Not until the bell rings</u> can anyone leave the room. You must all remain here until then, even if you've finished the exam.

   ❑ emphasis   ❑ contrast of the structure   ❑ focus on the delayed subject

10. <u>Only when his wife is on a business trip</u> does he do any housework. Normally, he doesn't seem to notice what happens to the dirty dishes.

_____❑ emphasis   ❑ contrast of the structure   ❑ focus on the delayed subject

---

EXERCISE 8   (Focus 6)

In each of these brief dialogues there is something wrong with the form of the statement or the use in context of the second speaker. Determine whether the problem is one of form or use. Correct errors in form and explain problems with usage.

1. **Receptionist:** A single room is $750 plus tax, not including breakfast.

   Tourist: I have nowhere heard of such high prices.

   _____

   _____

2. **Teacher:** Have you forgotten what we studied yesterday?

   Student: Scarcely had you mentioned it when I forgot.

   _____

   _____

3. **Flight attendant:** Is there something wrong with your chicken, sir?

   Airline traveler: Little do you know I am a vegetarian.

   _____

   _____

4. **Doctor:** What can I do for you today?

   Patient: You must help me, doctor. Never I have been in such pain before.

   _____

   _____

5. **Police officer:** Do you know you were going 90 miles per hour? What's the rush?

   Motorist: No way am I going to be late for work.

   _____

   _____

6. **Doctor:** I would recommend a cortisone injection if you want to get rid of that condition quickly.

   Patient: Not under any circumstances I can take cortisone. I'm afraid I'm allergic to it.

   _____

   _____

Focusing and Emphasizing Structures:
It-Clefts and
Wh-Clefts

EXERCISE 1 (*Focus 1*)

The columns below consist of general knowledge information. Match the focus element with the appropriate clause and then make a complete sentence beginning with It + *be*, and linking the two elements with *that*, *who*, or *where*. Make any other necessary changes.

EXAMPLE: *It was Florence that led the Renaissance in the arts.* (3,g)

1. Carl Jung
2. Chicago
3. Florence
4. Marco Polo
5. Versailles
6. the Wright Brothers
7. China
8. the Black Death
9. Wyoming
10. the Haj

a. reached China during the rule of Kublai Khan.
b. made the first successful flight in a gasoline-powered aircraft.
c. is the pilgrimage to the holy city of Mecca during the twelfth month of the Islamic year.
d. the first book was printed.
e. developed the psychoanalytical theory of archetypes.
f. is the most rural state in the U.S.
g. led the Renaissance in the arts.
h. the treaty that ended World War I was signed.
i. the world's tallest building is located.
j. wiped out more than a third of Europe's population in the fourteenth century.

1. _____
2. _____
3. _____
4. _____
5. _____
6. _____
7. _____
8. _____

9. _____

10. _____

EXERCISE 2   (Focus 1)

Restate the following sentences using an _it_-cleft emphasis.

EXAMPLE: Some of the students in my Russian class are coming over this evening.

It is some of the students in my Russian class who are coming over
this evening.

1. Thoreau lived at Walden Pond, not Emerson.

_____

_____

2. The students have the responsibility to ask questions.

_____

_____

3. In Toledo our car broke down.

_____

_____

4. His thoughts of his children get him through his long working days.

_____

_____

5. Our cat didn't kill your bird.

_____

_____

6. Marjorie will pick up the cake.

_____

_____

7. Ivor must have taken the book.

_____

_____

8. My aunt has appeared in a movie.

_____

_____

9. You need to catch the number three bus. (emphasize the object)

_____

_____

10. I ordered shrimp, not steak. (emphasize the first object)

_____

_____

_____

EXERCISE 3   (*Focus 2*)

Restate the following sentences about the discoveries and events that led to the creation of the atom bomb to emphasize the information indicated in parentheses. Change any other wording as necessary. The first one has been done as an example.

1. Leo Szilard, a Hungarian physicist who had left Nazi Germany, realized the possibility of setting up a nuclear chain reaction in 1933. (emphasize the date.)

It was in 1933 that Leo Szilard, a Hungarian physicist who had left Nazi

Germany, realized the possibility of setting up a nuclear chain reaction.

2. In the winter of 1938, the German scientists Otto Hahn and Fritz Strassman demonstrated the process of nuclear fission. (emphasize the scientists)

_____

_____

3. In 1939 Albert Einstein wrote a letter to President Roosevelt to inform him about recent discoveries concerning uranium and also about the possibility of constructing a powerful bomb. (emphasize the purpose)

_____

_____

4. In August 1942, the top-secret Manhattan project was established to develop an explosive device based on nuclear fission. (emphasize the purpose)

_____

_____

5. On December 2, 1942, Enrico Fermi and his colleagues produced the first controlled nuclear reaction in a squash court beneath the stands of an abandoned football field at the University of Chicago. (emphasize the place)

_____

_____

6. In 1943, the Army chose J. Robert Oppenheimer to direct the lab in Los Alamos, New Mexico, where the atomic bombs would be designed and assembled. (emphasize the director)

_____

_____

7. The uranium and plutonium for the bombs was produced by huge reactors and separator plants in Washington and Tennessee. (emphasize the production facilities)

_____

_____

8. The first atomic bomb was detonated near Alamogordo, New Mexico, on July 16, 1945. (emphasize the date)

_____

_____

EXERCISE 4   (Focus 3)

Imagine that each of the following situations is true. Provide an explanation, either serious or humorous, emphasizing the reason. The first one has been done as an example.

1. Your mother doesn't receive a phone call from you on Mother's Day.

   It's because the lines were busy that I couldn't get through.

2. You receive a notice from the library informing you of books overdue one month.

   _____

   _____

3. You didn't receive the grade you wanted on your last English exam.

   _____

   _____

4. Someone points out that you are wearing two socks of completely different styles.

   _____

   _____

5. You can't make it to class today.

   _____

   _____

6. A friend asks you why you were caught speeding.

   _____

Answer the questions by naming a person in your family or circle of friends who best matches the following descriptions. Use a cleft sentence beginning with "it is" (or "it's") in your response.

EXAMPLE: Who tends to send everyone a birthday card?

It's my sister-in-law Meg who tends to send everyone a birthday card.

1. Who is the most practical?

_____

_____

2. Who tends to be a better listener than a talker?

_____

_____

3. Who tends to stay up late at night?

_____

_____

4. Who has traveled to more countries than anyone else?

_____

_____

5. Who would be most likely to clean up a messy room?

_____

_____

6. Who tends to be well-informed about politics?

_____

_____

7. Who most enjoys eating?

_____

_____

8. Who is in the best physical condition?

_____

_____

Choose a word from the list for a focus element and complete each blank so that the sentence is a cleft construction. The first has been done for you as an example.

inspiration   a drought

revenge   stagefright

stamina   memory

1. <u>It is revenge</u> that often provokes a vicious circle in response to an initial wrongdoing.

2. _____ that enables an athlete to endure even when he or she has little energy left.

3. _____ that is tragically lost due to Alzheimer's disease.

4. _____ that prevented the award winner from giving a speech at the banquet.

5. _____ that accounts for a creative person's new ideas.

6. _____ that drove many to abandon their homes in Oklahoma and move to California in the 1930s.

The following sentences explain either the causes or the effects of an action. Use a cleft construction with the appropriate tense and either *out of* (reason) or *for* (purpose) plus a word from the list to complete them. The first has been done as an example.

glory   frustration

malice   his country

generosity   a sense of honor

1. <u>It is for glory</u> that many rulers have set out to conquer neighboring lands.

2. _____ that many young men joined the army in World War I and not because they truly wished to fight.

3. _____ that many people donate large sums of money to charitable causes.

4. _____ that the gang of boys threw stones at the starving dog.

5. _____ that Nathan Hale, an American patriot hanged by the British, said he was giving his life.

6. _____ that the writer threw down his pen after sitting at his desk for an hour without having produced one interesting sentence.

   You have been asked to edit a reference book manuscript for errors. Unfortunately, much of the book turns out to be a treasury of misinformation. As you read each fact, identify the part that is incorrect. Make up a statement indicating what needs to be corrected, using a cleft sentence to highlight that element.

   EXAMPLE: Situated in the Andes range, K2, at 28,250 feet, is the world's second highest peak.

   Correction: *It is in the Karakoram range that K2 is situated.*

1. Harrison Ford starred in the first half dozen James Bond films.

   Correction:_____

   _____

2. Zambia is the country directly to the north of South Africa.

   Correction:_____

   _____

3. The election of 1860 of an anti-slavery candidate, Thomas Jefferson, as President prompted seven southern states to break away from the Union, an action that led to civil war.

   Correction:_____

   _____

4. The cerebrum makes up two-thirds of the entire heart and is divided into two interconnected halves, or hemispheres.

   Correction:_____

   _____

5. *The Werewolf of London* is a novel by Mary Shelley about a scientist who brings to life a hideous suffering creature without a sense of good and evil who finally kills his creator.

   Correction:_____

   _____

6. Between 1519 and 1521, Francisco Pizarro conquered Mexico and ended the Aztec Empire.

   Correction:_____

   _____

7. A person given a virus is made immune to the disease and cannot pass it on to anyone else.

   Correction:_____

   _____

8. In 1445, Johann Gutenberg published the complete works of Shakespeare, the first printed book in Europe.

Correction:_____

_____

9. The game of backgammon ends by checkmate, a term from the Persian "shah mat," which means the king is dead.

Correction:_____

_____

EXERCISE 9   (Focus 4)

Choose one feature to highlight among the following historical facts and write an introductory sentence for a historical narrative about each person.

EXAMPLE: It was in 485 B.C. that Cincinnatus took command and rescued the

Roman army.

PERSON	DATE	PLACE	EVENT
Cincinnatus (leader)	485 B.C.	Rome	takes command and rescues army surrounded by enemy
Mohammed (prophet)	622	Arabia	flees Mecca for Medina
Ashot I (ruler)	859	Armenia	founds Bagratide dynasty
Marco Polo (traveler)	1298	Genoa	begins to dictate his memoirs in jail
Francis Drake (explorer, pirate)	1581	England	returns from voyage of circumnavigation
Beethoven (composer)	1792	Vienna	becomes Haydn's pupil
Frank Whittle (inventor)	1937	England	builds first jet engine

1. _____

2. _____

3. _____

4. _____

5. _____

6. _____

7. _____

Choose one feature among the following facts to highlight and write an introductory sentence for a journalistic narrative about each person.

EXAMPLE: It is on a cold day in June in Patagonia that biologist Grace Snyder sets out to visit an unmapped valley.

PERSON	TIME	PLACE	EVENT
Grace Snyder (biologist)	cold day in June	Patagonia	sets out to visit an unmapped valley
John le Carré (writer)	just after midnight	Istanbul	plane lands
Jacques Cousteau (oceanographer)	at dawn	the Red Sea	prepares to dive
Peter Hillary (mountaineer)	during an avalanche	Mt. Makalu in the Himalayas	wonders if he should retire
Colin Bragg (gangster)	one day in February	Nassau	suddenly disappears
Tsering Paldum (medical researcher)	at the end of a long and intense week	Sloan Institute	first notices rapid changes in a fungal culture

1. _____

2. _____

3. _____

4. _____

5. _____

Make up a cleft sentence for each situation that follows. The first has been done as an example.

1. You want to thank a friend for the great party that he gave last Saturday night.

   What a great party it was that you gave last Saturday!

   _____

2. You are busily taking notes in a medicine class as the lecturer explains how gamma globulin types differ. Someone behind you has a brief coughing fit and you miss what he says. Politely ask the instructor to go over the last point.

   _____

   _____

3. Yesterday your spouse asked you when the insurance payment is due. You said it was on the fifteenth. Today your spouse asks you if it is due on the sixteenth. Tell him/her what you said.

   _____

   _____

4. The telephone rings very late at night and wakes you up. Someone else in the house answers it. You wonder who could have been calling so late but you don't ask until the next morning.

   _____

   _____

5. You are listening to the weather report on the radio with your grandfather, whose hearing is not very good. The meteorologist has just said that rain is on the way because of a low pressure front coming in from the south. Your grandfather wants to know why it's going to rain. You tell him what the meteorologist said.

   _____

   _____

6. You are applying for financial aid at your college and an administrator gives you a form you've never seen before. You don't understand what you should fill out on the form. Ask her.

   _____

   _____

Match each phrase in Column A with an appropriate word or phrase from Column B. Connect them with an appropriate form of *be* and write the complete sentence in the space below.

EXAMPLE: <u>What Hamlet believed was that his uncle had murdered his father.</u>

(10, a)

A	B
1. What Kennedy said	a. that his uncle had murdered his father.
2. What made John D. Rockefeller rich	b. the computer
3. Where Tristan da Cunha is located	c. genetics
4. What covers most of the surface of the planet	d. a mystery
5. Who was crowned emperor on Christmas Day 800	e. "Ask not what your country can do for you, but what you can do for your country."
6. What makes revision easier	f. eat right and train every day
7. What accounts for certain characteristics	g. its canals
8. Who the man behind the iron mask was	h. water
9. What athletes have to do	i. oil
10. What Hamlet believed	j. Charlemagne
11. What Venice is noted for	k. in the middle of the South Atlantic Ocean

1. _____

2. _____

3. _____

4. _____

5. _____

6. _____

7. _____

8. _____

9. _____

10. _____

11. _____

Write in the teacher's portion of the dialogues by using a W*h*-cleft to correct the errors in the students' statements.

EXAMPLE: **Huda:** They speak French in the Philippines.

Teacher: _What they speak in the Philippines is Tagalog._

1.   **Pema:** A gerund follows the verb *forget*.
  Teacher: _____

2.   **Junko:** Muslims cannot eat lamb.
  Teacher: _____

3.   **Ned:** The Confederate army wore blue in the Civil War.
  Teacher: _____

4.   **Arvydas:** The Olympic Games started in Rome.
  Teacher: _____

5.   **Clem:** All children need punishment.
  Teacher: _____

6.   **Hans:** M*ust* indicates possibility.
  Teacher: _____

7.   **Nils:** Our galaxy is called Alpha Centaury.
  Teacher: _____

8.   **Ruta:** Vincent van Gogh wrote music.
  Teacher: _____

Test Preparation Exercises
Units 22–25

Choose the one word or phrase that best completes each sentence.

1. I guess you're right. Recycling makes sense. I certainly _____ start recycling.
   - (A) am
   - (B) will
   - (C) was
   - (D) do

2. _____ quiet, alert, and patient is essential to anyone wishing to observe animal behavior in the wild.
   - (A) In order to be
   - (B) That a person is
   - (C) That a person be
   - (D) That being

3. _____ that he kicked his car.
   - (A) It was for desperation
   - (B) It was out of desperation
   - (C) Out of desperation was it
   - (D) For desperation was it

4. _____ smile at the blunders of his youth and regard them as simple indiscretions.
   - (A) Not for anything could he
   - (B) Not for anything he could
   - (C) He could not make any
   - (D) Could he not make any

5. It was stipulated that a student _____ a grade point of not less than 3.0 in order to keep a scholarship.
   - (A) maintains
   - (B) maintain
   - (C) will maintain
   - (D) have to maintain

6. _____ anyone know that the old woman on the park bench had once been a famous actress.
   - (A) Little did
   - (B) Rarely has
   - (C) It was rare for
   - (D) Not only does

7. He ignored his doctor's recommendation _____ smoking cigarettes.
   - (A) about the stopping
   - (B) that must stop
   - (C) that he stops
   - (D) that he stop

8. No sooner had the island finished cleaning up the debris from the last hurricane _____ another ferocious storm struck.
   - (A) when only
   - (B) and
   - (C) then
   - (D) than

9. It _____ small victory for the community that there were no violent incidents in the high schools during all of last year.

        (A) was no   (C) did not have no

        (B) wasn't no   (D) did not have a

10. _____ that I stayed up long past my usual bedtime to finish it.

        (A) The book was suspenseful   (C) So suspenseful the book was

        (B) So suspenseful was the book   (D) In suspense was I

11. "The testimony sounds confused and a bit phony. I think the witness is lying."
"Sorry, but I really _____ believe you're mistaken."

        (A) can   (C) do

        (B) cannot   (D) did

12. The ad hoc committee insisted that the employees' cafeteria _____ fixed up immediately.

        (A) will be   (C) must

        (B) should   (D) be

13. _____ Hermann Hesse who won the Nobel Prize for Literature in 1946?

        (A) Was it   (C) Did not

        (B) That it was   (D) Not only

14. In no way _____ my opinion.

        (A) the new theory changes   (C) does change the new theory

        (B) changes the new theory   (D) does the new theory change

15. _____ precisely the mythical island of Atlantis was has not ever been clearly established.

        (A) That   (C) That was

        (B) Where   (D) It was

Identify the *one* underlined word or phrase that must be changed for the sentence to be grammatically correct.

16. The assistant manager's <u>recommendation</u> <u>that</u> the accountant <u>is fired</u> <u>was received</u> with
                          A   **B**   **C**   **D**
little enthusiasm.

17. <u>Not until</u> the end of the third Punic War in 146 B.C. <u>when Rome emerged victorious</u> over
    A   **B**
Carthage, <u>Rome could claim</u> to control the coast of North Africa in the region <u>that is now</u>
           C   **D**
<u>known</u> as the Maghreb.

18. <u>Better than</u> anyone <u>could have anticipated</u> <u>there was</u> the medal-winning performance of
    A   **B**   **C**
the figure skater and <u>only a short while</u> after a major injury.
                     D

19. What a stunning job is it they are doing now cleaning all the stained glass windows of
    A   **B**   **C**   **D**

Chartres cathedral.

20. Under no circumstances I would allow my seven-year-old to ride his bike to school along
         A   **B**   **C**   **D**

a busy highway.

21. That a tiny flea can actually jump with a thrust 140 times the force of gravity can be
    A   **B**   **C**

astonishing, to say the least.
           D

22. That is to Lakshmi, the goddess of abundance, fertility, and prosperity, that rural Hindus
    A   **B**   **C**

most often address their prayers.
      D

23. Tell your brother that it is absolutely critical that he drains last season's oil from his
                    A   **B**   **C**

power tools before using them this season.
               D

24. That many people, perhaps even today, have a hard time comprehending is how the
    A   **B**   **C**

planet can actually be traveling at a great speed through space while no one has the
                                                D

sensation of such velocity.

25. Never I could have imagined that the envelope contained the news that a distant uncle
      A   **B**   **C**

had left me fifty thousand dollars.
  D